DOMESTIC POLICY FORMATION _____

DOMESTIC POLICY FORMATION

Presidential-Congressional Partnership?

STEVEN A. SHULL

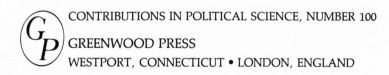

CONTRIBUTIONS IN POLITICAL SCIENCE, NUMBER 100

GREENWOOD PRESS

WESTPORT, CONNECTICUT • LONDON, ENGLAND

Library of Congress Cataloging in Publication Data

Shull, Steven A.
  Domestic policy formation.

  (Contributions in political science, ISSN 0147-1066 ;
no. 100)
  Bibliography: p.
  Includes index.
  1. Presidents—United States.   2. United States.
Congress.   3. Policy sciences.   I. Title.   II. Series.
JK585.S53   1983   353.03'72   82-24174
ISBN 0-313-23770-0 (lib. bdg.)

Library of Congress Catalog Card Number: 82-24174
ISBN: 0-313-23770-0
ISSN: 0147-1066

First published in 1983

Greenwood Press
A division of Congressional Information Service, Inc.
88 Post Road West
Westport, Connecticut 06881

Printed in the United States of America

10 9 8 7 6 5 4 3 2 1

DEDICATED to my wife, Janice, who in addition to providing me with a pleasant environment in which to work, assisted immeasurably with her skillful proofreading

Contents

Figures

Tables

Preface

The formation of domestic policy is an extremely complex process, often with unclear boundaries. This policy arena is dynamic and cyclical, containing observable stages within which the roles of the participants vary. I argue in this book that the process of policymaking depends upon the strategies and interactions of political actors and upon particular content (functional and substantive areas) of public policy. Thus, there are three components to this book: process, actors, and content in policymaking. Because the goal is explanation of the policymaking process, four stages of its formation are the units of analysis and provide the organizational basis for this book: agenda-setting, initiation, modification, and adoption.

The goal of empirically testing for the effects of actor interaction and policy content on the policy formation process makes it impossible to cover the universe of any of the three phenomena. Data availability and importance of their roles have led to the decision to focus on Congress and the President as the ultimate deciders (primary actors) in national policy formation. Also, although many overall comparisons will be made, the book concentrates on selected content areas of policy. These content areas are grouped according to three functional areas of Theodore Lowi's typology: distributive, regulatory, and redistributive. Even more important than this typology is the in-depth concentration on six substantive areas of policy subsumed within them: agricultural price supports, public works, crime, antitrust, civil rights, and poverty. If we can better understand actor interaction and policy content as they relate to the process of domestic policy formation in these areas, we will gain greater understanding of the policy process as a whole.

Apart from the overriding theme of explaining the policy process, this book seeks to address several subsidiary questions: (1) Can we identify and clarify roles in policy formation? (2) Do such variables as political party, time, and policy area relate to differences in actor emphasis and behavior? (3) Is the functional or substantive content of issues more important in predicting the policy process than the behavior of political actors? (4) Are actors rational and consistent? (5) Are we witnessing a decline in Presidential dominance in domestic policy formation, particularly in its latter stages? In prescribing recommendations, the focus in the concluding chapters is on the need for greater cooperation and accountability, since policy outputs seem to be influenced increasingly by actors now less subject to Presidential control.

This empirical investigation should answer some of these questions. In addressing Lowi's assertion that policy determines politics, the research systematically evaluates the validity and utility of his typology. Reciprocal causation is expected; the pattern of politics should influence policy choices, but so too should the type of policy affect the patterns of politics. Substantive categorizations should be even more powerful in explaining policy outputs. If these issues are successfully dealt with in the domestic policy arena, then we will add to our knowledge of the process and content of public policy, as well as understand the interaction of the primary actors in its formation.

In short, this book looks at the interplay between politics and public policy. All too often we see emphasis on one component at the expense of the other. If politics is important in policymaking (and vice-versa), political interactions are at the heart of domestic policy formation, for it is here that relations among political actors and institutions are most evident. The formative stage of domestic policy is highly visible and conflictual, requiring greater power sharing and accommodation than may be true elsewhere in the public policy arena. Presidents usually try to lead, as has been the norm since the 1930s, but the frequently posited Presidential preeminence model is by no means assured in the formation of domestic policy. Domestic policy formation is complex, fragile, and elusive; change often is difficult or attempted with great reluctance. Nevertheless, it is anticipated that both Congress and the President increasingly are seeking to effect change: Presidents particularly in agenda-setting and initiation, Congress especially in modification and adoption. Both actors have opportunities for influence at all stages—influence that is highly dependent on the general political climate. But because of characteristic conflict in domestic policy formation, skillful interaction and eventual cooperation are necessary if the policy goals of Congress and the President are to be achieved.

Because empirical studies encompassing many variables, relationships, and sources of data can become quite complex, a Methodological Appendix is provided for those who wish to delve more deeply into the analysis. The detailed explanation of variables and indicators is required for a comprehensive assessment of some of the measures. This book, in systematically examining changes in the process, content, and actor roles in domestic policy formation, performs a difficult task but an essential one for a fuller understanding of public policy.

Acknowledgments

A project of this magnitude is rarely the product of one person. While I absolve them of any blame, I do wish to credit several persons for their assistance, ranging from data collection to reading frequently very rough drafts of my chapters. While I prevailed on some friends to read virtually the entire book (Cohen, LeLoup, Ripley, J. Shull, Stewart, Thomas), many others deserve thanks for giving freely of their valuable time.

These friends and colleagues, listed alphabetically, include Jeffrey E. Cohen, Werner J. Feld, Grace A. Franklin, Edward V. Heck, Susan E. Howell, John R. Johannes, Thomas A. Kazee, John H. Kessel, Lance T. LeLoup, Michael D. McDonald, William S. Maddox, Morris S. Ogul, George E. Rawson, Randall B. Ripley, Janice K. Shull, Elliot E. Slotnick, Joseph Stewart Jr., Norman C. Thomas, and Stephen J. Wayne. Additionally, James T. Sabin, Vice President, Editorial, and Mildred Vasan, Senior Production Editor, at Greenwood, provided encouragement, competent reviews, and valuable advice on this book.

Over the course of this research I had the assistance of two superior graduate assistants, Albert Ringelstein, Jr. and Margaret Klemm. Four different typists worked ably on several drafts of this work: Betsy Rawson, Rosemary Johnson, Muriel Murphy, and Gail White. Financial support was provided by my Department, College of Liberal Arts organized research grants, and a grant from the UNO Graduate Research Council. To all of these individuals and organizations I offer my heartfelt thanks.

DOMESTIC POLICY FORMATION _____

Domestic Policy Arena 1

The overriding theme of this book is that the process of domestic policy formation is systematically affected by conscious choices among participants and by the content of policies under consideration. Thus there is a necessary interaction among process, content, and participants (actors) in public policy. The interplay among these concepts is not new in the public policy literature. Indeed there is growing recognition that researchers must examine these notions if they are to understand the entire policy arena (Ranney 1968; Shull 1979a). How policy is made affects the substance of the policy obtained (Donovan 1970, 34), and decision makers are the ones who make such determinations.

Because the three concepts are very broad, an explanation of what will be covered is desirable. Beginning with process, primarily routine decisions in the domestic realm of policy formation are examined. The research does not delve into implementation or evaluation. Although more is known about policy formation than about its implementation or evaluation, little information is available in the scholarly literature on the actual process of routine policy formation. What has appeared is essentially of two types: textual sources discussing the stages and/or substages of the policy process in a general (usually cursory) fashion, and case studies of policymaking in crises or in a particular substantive area of policy.[1]

In order to attain desired results, decision makers must first traverse several stages in the policymaking process. Four substages of policy formation are examined in this book: agenda-setting, initiation, modification, and adoption. Although the line separating these activities (or substages) is often blurred, the distinction is useful in understanding interactions in policymaking.

The organization of this book by process (Chapters 2-5) should not be construed as slighting policy content. Indeed, policy content (or substance) is posited as the primary explanatory variable in the analysis. Thus, the study allows a definitive examination of the assertion that the content of policy itself determines policy decisions (Lowi 1964, 1970; Ranney 1968; Salisbury and Heinz 1970).

Policy typologies or categorizations help explain differences in the content of public policy. Fairly broad substantive areas are examined and then narrowed into six policy groups: agricultural price supports, public works, crime, antitrust, civil rights, and poverty. Concrete examples and case studies illustrate the importance of these six groups. Analytical (or functional) typologies may also help explain actor emphases and behavior in the process of domestic policy formation. The widely cited functional typology developed by Theodore Lowi (1964) is also incorporated to organize the data and discussion. An empirical test of Lowi's typology should reveal whether the meaningful differences among distributive, regulatory, and redistributive policies claimed by its proponents exist. Although there has been debate over the utility of such policy categorizations, this examination should allow comparisons of the relative salience of substantive and functional typologies, and perhaps even their capability of predicting the policy process.

The goal of empirically testing for the effects of policy content and actor interaction on the policy formation process makes it impossible to cover the universe of any of the three phenomena. Data availability and pervasiveness of their roles make it imperative to focus on Congress and the President as the ultimate deciders in national policy formation. Influence is expected to result from skillful and effective interaction among actors in policy formation. Normally this involves such components of politics as successful bargaining, accommodation, and the minimizing of conflict. Rationality is assumed; actions at one stage are assumed to be consistent with their behavior at other stages in the policy process.

Domestic policy formation is anticipated to have changed greatly over the years. Once the province of Congress and subgovernments, agenda-setting and initiation have largely come under the purview of the institutionalized Presidency. (Recent interest in water policy by Presidents Jimmy Carter and Ronald Reagan illustrates this change.) But if Congress has actually initiated far less policy than previously, it still clearly plays a major and probably growing role in modifying and legitimizing (adopting) Presidential policy preferences. The relative influence of Congress and the President, then, is expected to differ widely across stages in the policy process and according to the policy content and the political environment. Concealed beneath this rubric of domestic policy should be variations in Presidential-Congressional behavior depending on issue content. Poverty policy, for example, should be more President oriented, while public works should evince more Congressional leadership.

What, then, do we hope to learn from this book? We should observe that the policy formation process is quite complex, with widely differing roles, emphases, and behavior from Congress and the President. Judgments about the rationality and consistency of such decision making should be possible. Further, a winnowing process is anticipated, with the broad general agenda issues being refined into specific policy outputs in policy adoption. Finally, the expectation is for some diminution of Presidential dominance in policy formation, a dominance that reached its zenith in the mid-1960s.

Apart from the overriding theme of explaining the policy process, this study seeks to address several subsidiary questions: (1) Can we identify and clarify roles in policy formation? (2) Do such conditions as political party, Presidential assertiveness, Congressional acquiescence, and time relate to differences in actor emphasis and behavior? (3) Is the functional or substantive content of issues more important in predicting the policy process than the behavior of political actors? (4) Are actors rational and consistent? (5) What conditions have contributed to an expected decline in Executive dominance in policy formation? (6) What changes are observable in the process, content, and actor roles in domestic policy formation?

POLICY PROCESS

Policy formation refers to the making of decisions to attain desired goals. This process is dynamic (ongoing but changing) and cyclical (recurrent and continuous). Such a characterization suggests sequential development of policy formation consisting of several subprocesses: identification of the problem, gathering of information, screening and weighing of the alternatives, and the approval of a preferred choice.

Authors have proposed different terms for describing essentially the same substages of policy formation. James Anderson (1979) and Anderson, David Brady, and Charles Bullock (1978, 8) use *formation* (which presumably is analogous to agenda-setting) and then *formulation* and *adoption*. Charles O. Jones (1977) adds the notion of legitimating programs, which suggests a larger role for Congress. Randall Ripley and Grace Franklin, in focusing on Congressional-bureaucratic interaction, combine formulation and legitimation (1980, 2). Nelson Polsby comes closest to the scheme presented in this book by subdividing policy formation into incubation, formulation, modification, and appraisal (1969, 66-68). The four substages incorporated here allow an assessment of actor interaction in policy formation, focusing primarily on Congress and the President.

Substages of Policy Formation

Agenda-setting establishes goals (and sometimes priorities). Usually it is in the form of rhetoric that calls attention to a problem. It sets forth a broad policy emphasis but does not necessarily advocate specific programs. Although agenda advocacy need not be very specific, it is designed to help other governmental actors see that a problem exists and to prepare them for action. The agenda, then, consists only of those issues that are to be addressed by governmental action (Anderson, Brady, and Bullock 1978, 8).

An issue usually reaches the public (government) agenda as a result of conflict over the allocation of resources. According to Robert Eyestone, an "issue arises when a public with a problem seeks or demands government action and there is public disagreement over the best solution to the problem" (1978, 3). Thus, conflict and its resolution generally influence what reaches the public agenda. In Charles Lindblom's words, "Agendas are determined by interaction among persons struggling with each other over the terms of their cooperation" (1980, 4). Although controversial issues are most likely to appear on the public agenda, so also are issues that affect a large number of persons (Cobb and Elder 1972, 152-53).[2] When the mass public becomes concerned over an issue, an infrequent occurrence, it almost invariably reaches the government agenda.

Agenda-setting merges with initiation (formulation) as policy initiatives are formally proposed. Initiation consists of more concrete "acquisitive" actions than merely "rhetorical" statements because means are developed for problem solving (see Ripley and Franklin 1975, 11, for a discussion of these terms). The term initiation suggests innovation, which seldom occurs in formulating policy; decision makers offer few totally new or innovative ideas. Thus, whatever actually may be wanted or said, usually only modest (small or incremental) change results. Even actions seemingly encompassing considerable change are seldom innovative.

Formulation often must proceed without the problem's being clearly defined. Nevertheless, alternative methods and a planned course of action constitute government's proposed solution to the problem. Many types of initiatives exist, including administrative rules, court opinions, and legislative proposals. As was the case with agenda-setting, the lines between initiation and later stages blur. The policies are formulated with an eye to how they will be modified and what compromises will be necessary to secure their adoption in the domestic policy arena.

Modification involves the assessment of the proposals formulated. Like the other substages considered here, modification has several components. It includes the selling of proposals through coalition building and the mobilization of group support, frequently involving the expenditure of considerable resources. Also included is the dissemination of information about the justification and intent of the proposed policy. During this process, policymakers will receive feedback from their constituents. Because proposals normally must pass through many decision stages, there are multiple points of access and opportunities for influence by both governmental and nongovernmental actors. Communicating policy preferences is the primary function in policy modification. Persuasion and bargaining, rather than command, frequently are more appropriate to this end (Anderson 1979; Neustadt 1980). Effective advocacy usually is necessary to inspire societal forces toward new policy directions. As with other substages, however, most modification also reflects little policy change, largely because actors have considered political feasibility in their agenda-setting and formulation decisions.

Adoption, the final substage of policy formation, requires accommodation among many participants and ultimate government approval. Because prior agreement or acquiescence need not lead to agreement on actual policy, the need continues to satisfy a multitude of demands. Building majority support (Congressional in this case) for public policies depends upon many conditions: support from nongovernmental actors, partisan composition of executive and legislative institutions, ideological conflict within and between these institutions, and the substantive policy issues under question.[3] Certainly adoption (governmental acceptance of the proposed solution) does constitute legitimation by elected representatives. Although the President can adopt some issues on his own (for example, through executive orders), Congress must authorize and appropriate funds for most policy items. Such legislative approval tells us a great deal about the strength, independence, and interaction of both actors.[4]

Why the Sequential Approach?

The discussion so far has suggested that the roles, emphases, and behavior of political actors vary across stages of the policy process. As should be readily apparent, fluidity is an important part of policymaking, which the sequential approach highlights. The sequential approach is advantageous in examining actor interactions to see whether rhetoric translates into action and then to observe whether legislative action is congruent with executive policy preferences. At the same time, the approach avoids rigidly assigning specific functions to particular actors. By emphasizing interaction among actors, the sequential approach also lends itself to meaningful comparisons across and between substantive policy areas (Anderson, Brady, and Bullock 1978, 12). Because policy often is chronological and not static, many writers have used the sequential approach to emphasize its fluid, cyclical nature.[5]

Advantages of the sequential approach are mitigated somewhat by its tendency to oversimplify the enormously complex policy formation process. Policy sometimes emerges without a clear

Figure 1-1. Policy Formation Process

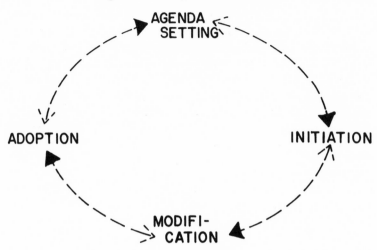

beginning or end and frequently is not as orderly or rational as a literal interpretation of the sequential approach may imply. Critics of the chronological approach contend that it encourages the assumption of a rational process "with each part logically tied to each succeeding part" (Lindblom 1980, 4). Lindblom goes further to argue that the actors, strategies, and issues do not vary much across the policy stages (1980, 3).

Acceptance of some of these criticisms as valid need not require rejection of the sequential scheme of policy formation, which, incidentally, may have even more validity than when used to encompass the entire policy process (including implementation and evaluation). Certainly we cannot draw neat lines between the point where one substage ends and another begins, and it probably matters little that we cannot (Jones 1977, 59). The process of policy formation should be thought of as fluid, as depicted in Figure 1-1, where there are primary one-way relationships, but where reciprocal relationships can also occur. Indeed, each substage can occur at different times. For example, another problem frequently reaches the agenda before the previous one is adopted, or the agenda may be modified before it is actually formulated. Thus, the sequential approach to policy formation probably has considerable utility when boundary and other conceptual difficulties are accounted for.

POLICY CONTENT

In addition to identifying the early substages of the policy process, policy formation may be analyzed according to content areas. Content refers to the function or substance of the policies themselves. Examples of functional areas authors have used include distributive and symbolic; examples of substantive areas include defense and civil rights. It is hypothesized here that variations in the content of policies under consideration produce variations in the roles and behavior of actors. This is due partly to the assertion that actors perceive differences among types of policies (Clausen 1973; Kessel 1974). Agreement on the meaning of policy among actors helps structure their emphasis in policymaking and suggests that observed differences in behavior may be attributable to the type of policy under consideration. Both functional and substantive typologies are used to ascertain whether differing processes and actor interactions are at work.

Empirical and/or theoretical differences in policies have been found in both the legislative and executive spheres.[6] Research at the national level has discerned that both Congress and the President perceive domestic policy according to at least four substantive areas: social benefits, civil rights, government management, and agriculture-natural resources (Clausen 1973; Kessel 1974; LeLoup and Shull 1979a). The substantive policy areas to be incorporated here include all of these broad dimensions of domestic policy, as well as narrower subissues.

One may also categorize policy according to functional areas. Functional categorizations usually group policy outcomes in some theoretically interesting way rather than according to the substance of issues themselves. Numerous scholars have justified such typologies theoretically (Lowi 1964; Edelman 1974; Froman 1968; Salisbury and Heinz 1970). A functional typology first advanced by Lowi in 1964 is perhaps the most popular and has been adopted widely.[7] Lowi categorized policies as distributive, regulatory, or redistributive depending upon their relative coercion and impact on society.[8]

Functional Typology

The Lowi typology is used in this examination of Presidential and Congressional roles in policymaking. A conceptual treatment of the properties of the three categories follows. The data incorporated not only indicate actor focus and behavior in policy formation but should also allow us to ascertain the discriminating value of Lowi's functional classification scheme.

Distributive policies primarily affect specific, homogeneous groups of the citizenry (Chandler, Chandler, and Vogler 1974, 110). They arise from relatively narrow issues and provide mostly individualized, short-run benefits. These features give distributive policies rather low visibility, which results in little conflict in the policy process (Lowi 1970, 321). Examples of distributive issues include agricultural price supports, public works, and most construction and research and development activities by government. Distributive policies are determined for the most part by individuals and small groups in Congress (such as subcommittees) with little Presidential but often lower-level executive branch involvement. Logrolling characterizes distributive policymaking because such policies constitute many routine decisions affecting primarily small groups. This decision style is most conducive to a powerful role by Congress (Orfield 1975, 261), and Presidential cooperation or even acquiescence seems to dominate these policies (Lowi 1972, 305-8; Ripley and Franklin 1980, 213).

Regulatory policy involves the application of general rules to specific decisions. Sanctions or restrictions (that is, greater coercion) characterize regulatory policies although benefits may also be conferred. Regulations tend to involve broad extensions of governmental control that affect large elements of society. Crime, pollution, and antitrust are examples of regulatory policies. Regulatory policy issues generally are more visible, less stable, and more conflictual than distributive policy issues (Vogler 1977). Congress as an institution probably is the major actor (Lowi 1972, 306), but collaboration with the Supreme Court and the executive branch (particularly the bureaucracy) is necessary and critical because of the highly technical nature of many regulatory issues.

Redistributive policies allocate benefits and impose costs by taking from one group and giving to another. Thus, some groups win while others must lose. These policies generally have the broadest impact on society.[9] Aaron Wildavsky (1979, 377-83) sees the degree of equality as defining the redistributive nature of policy. Civil rights (such as school desegregation) and poverty (such as subsidized housing) are among issues defined as redistributive. (See Table A-1 in the Appendix for examples of issues categorized into these three groupings.) Redistributive policies often alienate powerful interests and lead to political instability (Lowi 1964, 707; Chandler, Chandler, and Vogler 1974, 111). Accordingly, Congress tends to be reluctant to undertake such rearrangement. Both Presidential discretion and conflict with Congress are greatest in redistributive policies and least in the distributive area (Vogler 1977, 310). This is largely because the former is much more ideological than the latter (Ripley and Franklin 1982). The impetus for redistributive policy usually comes from the President.

This discussion of Lowi's three policy types is summarized diagrammatically in Figure 1-2. The defining characteristics are viewed along a continuum ranging generally from low on distributive to high on redistributive. Normally, regulatory issues fall between the two extremes. It is primarily the relationship between Congress and the President (No. 5-6 in Figure 1-2) that is of present concern, however. The study hopes to establish that the two actors differ in their roles, their emphasis on policy issues, and their behavior in both the process and content of policy formation.

Figure 1-2. Characteristics of Lowi's Policy Typology

DISTRIBUTIVE	REGULATORY	REDISTRIBUTIVE
Low	Moderate	High

Characteristics:

1. Visibility
2. Number of people affected
3. Instability
4. Innovativeness
5. Presidential dominance/emphasis
6. Conflict between Congress and President
7. Ideological disputes

Substantive Typology

The Lowi functional areas are quite broad and provide the starting point for examining policy content. The six substantive areas incorporated are an amalgamation of Lowi's on one hand and those mentioned previously by Aage Clausen and John Kessel on the other. The Clausen-Kessel areas (agricultural assistance, natural resources, government management, civil rights and liberties, and social benefits) do not perfectly fit Lowi, so by choosing somewhat more specific types that do fit more closely we can better understand both functional and substantive areas.[10] Thus, we begin with more general policy and then gradually work toward understanding more specific issues. All policy requires some intellectual ordering; level of generality is a good way to sort things out.

The various levels of generality to be examined appear in Table 1-1. Such disaggregation allows in-depth investigation of policy content and also manageability in the various data to be used. At the same time, subissues at least through Level IV in Table 1-1 are probably still broad enough to allow quantitative analysis. The designations by Congressional Quarterly are used as the basis for the fit of subissues to broader substantive categorizations. (The list of key words defining each substantive area and corresponding discussion of these levels in Table 1-1 appear in the Methodological Appendix, Table A-2.) The substantive issues focused upon appear typical of the three types of policy Lowi identifies.

All of the substantive areas were chosen primarily for their visibility and political salience. Both governmental and nongovernmental actors have shown interest in each of these policy areas. Some public opinion and interest group data are available, as are measures of the Congressional and Presidential activity that occurs in each. The behavior of the latter should vary considerably across the six areas. The fact that some of these policy areas have frequently been controversial may not allow generalization across all government programs, but they are at the cutting edge of politics by virtue of controversy and perceived high stakes. Thus, comparisons among and between these issues should be a useful step in understanding policy formation.

ACTORS IN POLICY FORMATION

The assumption here is that the two most crucial participants in policy formation are Congress and the President, but other actors can be important too. We have seen considerable change during the twentieth century in the roles played by all participants, with ebbing and flowing of resources and constraints. If other actors are

Table 1-1. Substantive and Functional Areas

		Distributive	Regulatory	Redistributive
GENERAL	I.	Distributive	Regulatory	Redistributive
	II.	Agriculture, Natural Resources	General Government, Economic Management	Social Benefits, Civil Rights and Liberties
	III.	Price Supports, Public Works	Crime, Antitrust	Poverty, Civil Rights
	IV.	Acreage Allotments, Water Projects	Organized Crime Control, Enforcement Provisions of Clayton Act	Federal Housing, School Desegregation
SPECIFIC	V.[a]	Parity for Cotton, Tenn-Tombigbee Project	Wiretapping of Crime Figures, Business Mergers	Busing, Rent Subsidies

a. Level V discussed intermittently.

important in policymaking, why does this book concentrate on Congress and the President? Because policy formation is at the beginning of the entire policy process, political leadership is often required to define and put forth program emphasis. But does this necessitate a minimal role for the courts, bureaucracy, or nongovernmental actors?

Anderson provides a useful way of understanding why Congress and the President are most important in policy formation. He considers them the primary actors, having the constitutional authority to act. Anderson also includes the courts, but they are not utilized here because of the perception that their role is greater in later rather than earlier stages of the policy process. Supplemental policymakers (such as agencies and appointed officials) obtain their authority from the primary actors and thus are potentially controllable by them (1979, 35). A third group of unofficial (nongovernmental) actors, such as interest groups and public opinion, possess no legal authority in policymaking (Anderson 1979, 41). Certainly legal authority is not the only criterion for leadership in policymaking, but such authority seems more germane to earlier than to later stages in the process.

The number of actual primary policymakers is quite small since ultimate power remains largely in the hands of an elected elite and their appointees. While interest groups have varied levels of input on policy formation, the public itself seldom seems to be a dominant influence (Edwards and Sharkansky 1978, 53; Light 1982, 93; Lindblom 1980, 121). Where policymakers are determined, little control is possible from nongovernmental actors. Despite increases in power to Presidents resulting from Congressional delegation, the process of policy formation is almost never a one-person show. The complexity of the process places much of its activities beyond Presidential control (Hofferbert 1974, 47). Although they seldom command, Presidents have considerable latitude over the timing of their actions.[11] Conflict or cooperation, or both, characterizes much of the interaction between Congress and the President, interaction that occurs at each substage of policy formation.

Roles in the Policy Process

This book asserts that the Executive is involved most in agenda-setting and policy initiation, and the role of Congress is greater in modification and adoption (Redford 1969, 124). Congress expects the President to set forth and advocate programs, as witnessed in its dismay over Eisenhower's failure to do so in 1953 (Neustadt 1955, 1015). Congress perceives its own role as working over these proposals at a later date. Our task now is to examine these substage interactions between Congress and the President more closely.

Agenda-Setting

We have seen the public agenda as "items receiving active and serious consideration by important policymakers" (Edwards and Sharkansky 1978, 100). Agenda issues come from many groups such as political parties, interest groups, the media, and larger societal forces and motivations. An example is the push by right-to-life groups for a constitutional amendment banning abortions. But groups must have access in order to have a problem considered for the public agenda, and that is where the President and Congress come in. Although getting on the government's agenda frequently is the result of many diverse environmental circumstances, the President stands at center stage. As seen by James MacGregor Burns:

Presidential government is a superb planning institution. The President has the attention of the country, the administrative tools, the command of information, and the fiscal resources that are necessary for intelligent planning, and he is gaining the institutional power that will make such planning operational. Better than any other human instrumentality he can order the relations of his ends and means, alter existing institutions and procedures or create new ones, calculate the consequences of different policies, experiment with various methods, control the timing of action, anticipate the reactions of affected interests, and conciliate them or at least mediate among them. [1965, 339]

Even if this position now seems overstated, the President is important in agenda-setting because of his role in stating and ranking policy issues. When innovation occurs (an infrequent happening), it comes from the Presidency in the agenda-setting stage. Instances of Presidential activism abound, including President Lyndon Johnson's use of task forces to bypass the bureaucracy and to set agendas in poverty policy. But we should remember that agenda items may also result from followership rather than overt leadership from elected officials. Proposition 13 in California and the subsequently broader tax revolt is one prominent example.

Since many public issues require legislative action, much of the President's agenda transfers to Congress. Congress occasionally is important in agenda-setting, and increasingly it has put forth many items on its own, such as area redevelopment and environmental pollution. Although its role is greater in formulation and later stages, Congress is next most important to the President and his staff in creating and defining issues for the public agenda (Bauer, Pool, and Dexter 1972).

Although there are many forums for government's agenda, the main one considered here is public expressions by the President, regardless of where an issue actually originated. Presidential statements, usually calling for legislative action, are the data used to determine which problems actually become political issues. Although issues reach Congress by other means, the President's public concerns almost automatically reach, and may even largely determine, the legislative agenda (Anderson 1979, 57; Lindblom 1980, 60; Redford 1969, 124).

Initiation

Presidents have a far greater role in initiating national policies in the twentieth century than they did previously. Perhaps because of the relative ease of proposing rather than implementing or evaluating, Presidents come to believe that initiating programs is the best way to assert their leadership and to make a distinctive mark in history. Although Richard Neustadt calls the President the "Great Initiator," any President finds other actors asserting important roles in policy formulation.

Since formulation is the proposal for a course of action, the President necessarily becomes the primary initiator (Anderson 1979, 63; Hofferbert 1974, 45). Most initiatives, however, actually well up from administrative agencies or decision-making bodies. Although Congress also initiates on its own, it is heavily reliant upon Executive leadership (Lindblom 1980, 60). Presidential initiatives give Congress a base with which to work, without which Congress has a difficult time producing unified policy alternatives (Jones 1977, 79).

Disagreement abounds over the ability of Congress to initiate policy. Some writers have charged that policy initiation is a function that Congress increasingly is unwilling and unable to perform. According to one researcher, the fragmented and diffuse nature of Congress cannot allow it to compete with the President as

Chief Initiator (Gallagher 1974, 231). Others argue, however, that Congress is not powerless in policy formulation; it still shares power approximately equally with the President (Chamberlain 1946; Moe and Teel 1970; Schwarz and Shaw 1976).

The notion that only the Executive can initiate policy today oversimplifies reality. Even though much initiation takes place in the executive branch (probably between 70 and 80 percent), "the content of the initiated proposals . . . [has probably] been influenced by policy demands from within the legislature" (Schwarz and Shaw 1976, 196). Congress, in fact, seems to be the most powerful competitor of the President in the determination of programs and priorities and increasingly is involved in executive decision making too. Numerous Presidential powers related to initiation (such as the veto, central clearance, and budgetary leadership) increasingly have become subject to Congressional challenge. Congress, then, plays a more important role in formulation than often is recognized, certainly with respect to the specific policies initiated, if not in setting broader national goals.

Evidence of policy formulation by the President can be obtained from his initiatives to Congress (specific Presidential proposals), showing whether the President follows through on his agenda statements. Although we would expect Presidential statements to translate into subsequent actions, legislative initiatives and budget requests require more commitment and the making of hard choices than do mere public statements.

Presidential initiatives to Congress are important indicators of the policy role of the Chief Executive. Although they do not provide a complete picture, they reflect concrete actions taken to carry out his priorities. The initiatives themselves tell us something about a President's level of activity (the volume of initiatives), as well as his policy interests and priorities (the relative distribution of initiatives). It is easy to compare the requests of Presidents from year to year and across administrations. Very little research, however, has probed beyond the numbers and delved into the substance of policy initiatives. That task is begun here.

Modification

Modification refers here to potential, if not actual, legislative scrutiny of Presidential policies. If agenda-setting and initiation are dominated largely by the President, modification and adoption are much more under the purview of Congress (Jones 1977, 94). Congress has many opportunities to place its stamp on, greatly redefine, or reject Presidential initiatives. The decentralized, diffused nature of power in Congress requires constant majority building by the President if he is to receive only limited tampering with his initiatives. Although he has persuasive powers, he communicates his views to Congress primarily through public messages and legislative liaison. Indeed, the quality of liaison operations probably has a great deal to do with the degree of legislative modification. The chaotic nature of liaison during President Carter's first two years surely contributed to his inability to obtain his desired policy preferences (Ripley and Franklin 1980, 54-55; Davis 1979).

Congress frequently has different predispositions from the President. It also has many ways of monitoring executive proposals, including committee hearings, legislative veto provisions, administrative oversight, and committee and floor amendments. While a number of these techniques are discussed, the scrutiny of Presidential positions on legislation is paramount. The extent to which Congress modifies Presidential preferences depends upon many factors in the political environment. Party affiliations of Congress and the President, constituency views and reelection prospects, and the perceived views of interest groups, the media, and the general public are among the more important conditions affecting Congressional modification.

Other participants may also play a role in policy modification where the frequently laborious legislative process provides numerous opportunities. The Administration will make its views known to Congress through liaison and committee testimony. The latter is also the major but not the sole point of access to Congress for the bureaucracy and interest groups. But because Congress controls access to many of its forums, it can limit or encourage these inputs into its modification activities.

Adoption

Congress must approve legislation, with the President relegated to the formal task of signing or vetoing bills. Only occasionally can he shape them to his will. Thus, one of the biggest hurdles a President now faces is getting Congress to accept Presidential policy initiatives. A primary manifestation of his leadership over Congress is the extent to which it gives the President what he wants.

With its ability to override Presidential vetoes of adopted policies too divergent from its preferences, Congress is the ultimate decider of most domestic policies. It is asserting its independence through greater scrutiny of policy initiatives from Presidents and other sources. Although there are varied pressures on Congressional decision making, it is gaining the capability to play a leadership role in adoption, not insulated from these pressures, but better able to obtain a more comprehensive picture of policymaking overall and its ramifications.

Approval of Presidential initiatives provides information about both the Congress and the President. Comparisons across policy areas may suggest arenas of Presidential strength vis-à-vis Congress, and, conversely, arenas of Congressional independence. Comparisons across party, Administration, and time provide a view of changes in Presidential strength or weakness in dealing with Congress. The imperfections of this kind of scorecard are well documented.[12] Yet Congressional approval of Presidential initiatives remains a useful set of data when used in the proper context. Probably most important, the data indicate how successful Presidents have been in obtaining support for their proposals from Congress and reveal the extent that adopted policies deviate from the original agenda.

Expectations in the Policy Process

Despite caution and difficulty of change in domestic policy formation, we normally expect Presidents to try to exert leadership early and Congress to respond. We have asserted generally decreasing influence of the President relative to Congress as the policy process unfolds from agenda-setting through adoption. Thus, Presidential influence is usually opposite the strength of Congress in each substage. Accommodation is necessary at each step, but the period since the 1960s suggests more conflict than cooperation. Generally Presidents who cooperate with Congress should have greater legislative success, but success also is dependent upon both the internal and external social, economic, and political environment.

Whether the President can exert leadership over Congress is related to many phenomena. Various environmental conditions suggest that actor perceptions are important. Presidential personality, the extent to which he seeks innovative change, the nature of economy and the times in general, the timing of Presidential proposals, the quality of his liaison staff, his previous experience, the extent to which he becomes involved personally, the degree of Congressional assertiveness, and the partisan and leadership composition of Congress may all be important in assessing actor interactions in the policy formation process.

With respect to personal involvement, several propositions seem plausible. Because legislation is an important way to formulate policy, especially in the domestic sphere, it seems reasonable to assert that Presidents will use legislative initiatives to enhance their influence. Thus, Presidential attention early in policy formation should help his influence later. In short, Presidents who actively articulate an agenda and propose legislative initiatives may be subject to considerable legislative modification but also should attain substantial legislative success.

Expectations across Content Areas

Overview

The substantive and/or functional content of the policy under consideration affects both the policy process and actor roles and expectations. Because the six substantive areas considered are also under the rubric of the functional typology, we expect actor roles to correspond to those asserted for each category. Distributive policy (for example, price supports and public works) should be more Congress oriented, partly because of the influence of subgovernments, while redistributive issues (such as civil rights and poverty) are more President oriented. The entire domestic policy arena is probably more conflictual than it once was (Wildavsky 1966; LeLoup and Shull 1979a; Shull 1979a, Ch. 10). Therefore, over time, increasing conflict may occur in each of the policy areas, partly because of more direct involvement by both the President and Congress. These actors share power roughly equally, and domestic legislation seems to be the primary battleground.[13]

Both Congress and the President focus on their areas of influence and expertise and seek to define issues accordingly. Presidents seem to prefer policies in areas where their influence is greatest and that have broader impact (Vogler 1977, 317). Reflecting its own interest, Congress tries to transform redistributive policies (such as the 1965 Elementary and Secondary Education Act) into distributive ones (Lowi 1972, 306).[14] Even conservative congressmen clamor for distributive programs. Such "bringing home the bacon" is helpful in reelection, while redistributive policies are less helpful (Fiorina and Noll 1979, 1098, 1101). Thus, distributive programs are probably the most likely to be initiated and to complete the process of policy formation.

It was asserted that the increasingly technical nature of society has necessitated a growth in regulatory policy.[15] This may have been largely at the expense of distributive issues, which dominated the policy arena in the nineteenth century (Lowi 1972, 300). Because of the level of expertise required, it is probable that a shift has occurred, moving policymaking in general and regulatory policy specifically from the legislative to the executive sphere (Vogler 1977, 304.) In a sense, both actors will be captured; Presidents will be required to emphasize regulatory measures more, and Congress increasingly will defer. The regulatory area and subareas such as crime and antitrust are expected to occupy an increasing share of the domestic policy arena over time.

Since redistributive issues tend to be controversial and ideological, normally it is the President, not Congress, who initiates policy in behalf of society's poor (Ripley and Franklin 1980; 183). The exception, of course, would be when conservative and/or inactive Presidents occupy the White House. Presidents Richard Nixon and Gerald Ford placed low priority on broad social reform. Because it requires a strong, assertive, and ideologically committed President to initiate redistributive policies (Lowi 1972, 302-3), programs reflecting a major redistributive change in existing policy are least likely to be initiated.

Distributive policies are less ideological than regulatory and redistributive issues in that they require fewer social rearrangements. Such issues as acreage allotments and water projects are more likely to be approved by Congress than are the more conflictual redistributive policies (Ripley and Franklin 1980, 230-31; Hayes 1978, 154). Congress is more sympathetic to distributive issues and will scrutinize them less intently (Fiorina and Noll 1979). Accordingly, Presidents should obtain greater approval on their distributive than on their regulatory and redistributive proposals.

Environmental Conditions

Environmental variables are also important in examining the content of policy. The extent to which Presidents choose to be active in policy formation is a crucial consideration. Also important is whether they desire expansion or contraction of government programs. Either of these preferences implies a change of considerable magnitude in policy from the status quo. Decision makers seldom offer totally new or innovative ideas; most policy formation builds heavily from existing programs (Wildavsky 1979, 65). To the extent that policy innovation does mean altering the nation's agenda, however, innovative policies (that is, vigorous actions to expand or contract) frequently occur with partisan or ideological changes in government, or both.

Democrats consistently are the party of domestic policy expansion, while the Republican party emphasizes contraction or the status quo (Wayne 1978, 19-20; McConnell 1976, 44). Certainly this was evident in the Nixon and Ford administrations. Whether it was due to ideology, Watergate, the growing magnitude of the federal deficit, the uncertain benefits and high costs of the social programs of the 1960s, or growing Congressional resurgence, the Nixon-Ford years generally represented the status quo. President Reagan has proved more active in pushing contractive policies than did his Republican predecessors.

There is probably also a partisan element in the propensity to emphasize particular policies, and expectations by party have already been hinted at. Based upon a wide variety of literature (Orfield 1975; Uslaner and Weber 1975; Fry and Winters 1970; Wayne 1978, 20), a relationship between party control of the Presidency and the tendency to initiate redistributive policies is expected. Specifically, Democratic Presidents should emphasize redistributive policies (such as civil rights and poverty programs) to a greater extent than do Republican Presidents.[16]

Presidents are expected to be more assertive during their first and last years in office and less so during reelection years (Light 1982, 41; Kessel 1975, 9). Not only are they less assertive during reelection years but they also receive less support from Congress at that time (Wayne 1978, 130). Thus, there should be less Congressional acquiescence during Presidential reelection years. The reasons for these expectations are simple. Although first year requires organizing and gaining experience in office, Presidents realize they must make their mark early while the honeymoon lasts. Thus, they should be most aggressive then and also when they are lame ducks. During this last year, they have greater freedom of action and presumably wish to leave a historical legacy. Election years differ because of their heightened political climate.

Redistributive policies tend to be expansive and to come earlier in Presidential terms; the later years of Presidents are more frequently characterized by contraction or the status quo (Nathan 1983). Since distributive policies "pass around the pork," it is probably a normal tendency for Presidents to initiate them if they are about to leave office, or, particularly, if they are seeking reelection. Thus, Presidents should emphasize redistributive policies during their first year and distributive policies in their last year, especially if they are running for reelection.

This chapter has outlined the basis for the process, content, and actor organization mechanism in studying domestic policy formation. This approach facilitates comparing roles, emphases, and behavior and assessing overall interaction and performance in the domestic policy arena. Limitations of the distinction among stages in the process and among substantive and functional areas of policy should be kept in mind. The complexity of the policy process can be observed as the wide range of early policy options narrows considerably; issues become less diffuse and more specific as the process unfolds.

Rhetorical statements by Presidents assert broad policy emphases, a type of agenda-setting. Presidential formulation is determined by the Executive's policy requests to Congress, the initiation of policy. Modification arises when legislative efforts are made to redefine Presidential actions, primarily through acceptance or rejection of his positions on legislation. The legislative success obtained by the President taps Congress's role in policy adoption. No one actor can control all of the stages, since policy formation normally requires examining alternatives developed by others. However, Presidential influence is important in agenda-setting and initiation, while Congress's influence is greatest in modification, adoption, and appraisal. Presidential influence, then, is greater in the beginning and middle stages of policy formation and that of Congress nearer the end. Although its role sometimes is important in issue formulation, Congress normally enters the policy formation process after some groundwork has been laid by the Executive.

This study introduces the domestic policy arena centered around Congress and the President. It examines empirically whether actor roles and influences differ across the substages of policy formation. Influence is expected to result from skillful interactions among participants in policy formation. Normally this involves successful bargaining, accommodation, and the minimizing of conflict. Presidential leadership should also be important, particularly if the Executive is personally active. Such active Presidents, normally Democrats, tend to push more policies and also policies that are expansive rather than contractive.

The President, and particularly his staff, are anticipated to play a growing role in policy formation since the 1950s and 1960s. It is also expected that Congress is more important than previously, especially in social policy (Orfield 1975, 187, 225). Congress has a growing list of sanctions that it is increasingly willing to impose on Presidents who do not recognize its importance in policy formation. It may be, as Erwin Hargrove (1974, 230) suggests, that the President would obtain greater success were he to involve Congress in an early and active role in agenda-setting.

Policy formation will be shown to have changed greatly over the years. Once the province of Congress and subgovernments, the process has largely come under the purview of the institutionalized Presidency. But if Congress has actually initiated far less than previously, it still clearly plays a major role in modifying and legitimizing Presidential policy preferences (Redford 1969, 124). The relative influence of Congress, the President, and other participants is expected to differ in each policy area. Concealed beneath this rubric of domestic policy are variations in Presidential-Congressional responses, depending on issue content.

The content of several domestic areas of policy is compared throughout the policy process. Public works, for example, is expected to be more Congress oriented, while poverty policy gets more Presidential attention and is therefore more President oriented. The study also hopes to ascertain whether policy content is more powerful than political actors or environmental variables in explaining the policy process. Policy content is observed in the form of both substantive and functional typologies, and we seek to ascertain the ability of such typologies to demarcate meaningful differences among policy areas.

Despite bold assertions about differences according to policy area, such typologies do not work magic. There is still ambiguity in policy, and, as seen in the Methodological Appendix, some of the conceptual and measurement problems, particularly in the Lowi scheme, are severe. Still, Peter Steinberger's assertion that they have no inherent meaning apart from actor perceptions (1980, 188-89) is not accepted; nor will Elinor Ostrom's (1980) argument that they are fatally flawed be without a fight.

Instead, we strive to flesh out the utility of admittedly sketchy and ambiguous typologies of policy. If Lowi is correct that policy-makers perceive inherent differences in types of policy, then his work is a genuine contribution to theory building in policymaking. If the typologies are as discriminating as their proponents claim, we should be able to discern differences in each of the policy areas and across time and policy stages. If such differentiation is possible, then the typologies will be useful in examining actor roles, perceptions, and behavior in public policy. Whether the functional or substantive areas prove more powerful, policy content may help explain the enormously complex actor interaction occurring in domestic policy formation.

NOTES

1. Textual sources include Anderson 1979; Anderson, Brady, and Bullock 1978; Jones 1977; MacRae and Wilde 1979. For case studies of decision making during crises, see McConnell 1963, and Allison 1971. Works examining particular decisions or areas of policy include Fritschler 1983; Rodgers and Bullock 1972; and Morgan 1970.

2. The many qualifiers in this paragraph are in recognition of the obvious exceptions in agenda-building, for example, where a small elite is successful in getting an item on the public agenda. Also, some issues are purposely kept off the agenda and therefore are nondecisions.

3. Jones, for example, sees the need for different actions for different programatic areas (1977, 124).

4. Although adoption of policies frequently is equated with actual decision making, the latter term is considered more inclusive here.

5. Sources utilizing the sequential approach include Jones 1977;

Anderson, Brady, and Bullock 1978; Anderson 1979; Shull 1979a; Polsby 1969, 66-68; and MacRae and Wilde 1979.

6. Other studies incorporating substantive typologies include LeLoup and Shull 1979b, Hofferbert 1974; Sharkansky 1970; Shull 1978, 1979a.

7. Examples of this utilization include Ripley and Franklin 1980, 1982; Vogler 1977; Uslaner and Weber 1975; Fry and Winters 1970; Spitzer 1979; Hayes 1978; Kessel 1977; Shull 1983b.

8. In later work, Lowi discussed a fourth policy type: constituent (1972, 300). Like distributive policy, constituent policy is characterized by little coercion. Logrolling also exists but is more partisan. This policy category is typified by such issues as reapportionment and creation of new agencies. It has not received much subsequent attention, however, and is excluded from the present effort. A different policy type (self-regulatory) has been offered by Salisbury and Heinz (1970), but it was omitted for essentially the same reason. I have not distinguished between competitive and protective regulation as do Ripley and Franklin (1982, 1980) but concede the utility of this differentiation.

9. This point is debatable. Because redistribution occurs less frequently (Hayes 1978), it could be argued that the more frequent distributive policies have greater impact on society.

10. Although the study draws on Lowi's functional areas and Clausen and Kessel's substantive areas, it does not fully test either typology.

11. Despite this popular interpretation, the thousands of executive orders are fairly close to commands.

12. For example, lumping all proposals together may not account for major policy initiatives. Spitzer 1979; Sigelman 1979; Wayne 1978, 168-71; Edwards 1980; Shull 1979a, 1981, all discuss problems with the Congressional Quarterly measures.

13. While foreign policy legislation constitutes an important proportion of Presidential initiatives (about 23 percent; see Shull 1979a, 212), executive orders and agreements, summit meetings, and crisis decision making often do not take the form of legislation. Indeed military and, especially, diplomatic policies frequently are made entirely without Congressional input. (Witness President Carter's 1977 pardon of draft resisters, his 1978 recognition of China, and his Middle East peacemaking role in 1979.)

14. There is some evidence that Congress is successful in doing just that. Problems occur in determining whether a policy is distributive or redistributive. Although a policy may be redistributive when adopted (for example, the Elementary and Secondary Education Act), it soon becomes distributive in that it is associated with incremental adjustments in benefits and the conflict that surrounded its initial adoption has subsided. If one says that the size of the economic stakes is the criterion, then it is

impossible to measure the impact of issues like busing or affirmative action. Thus, redistributive measures, once in place and accepted, tend to a political pattern similar to that which accompanies distributive policies. (Additional conceptual problems with the Lowi typology may be seen in the Methodological Appendix.)

15. The *National Journal* documents a tremendous surge of regulation beginning about 1970. Nearly half of the federal regulatory agencies have been established since then, and the number of pages in the *Federal Register* has more than tripled (January 19, 1980, 101).

16. One could argue that this expectation would depend greatly upon whether redistributive policies are major or minor. Congressional Quarterly contends that most major issues constitute more than one initiative, and therefore there is some weight for an issue's importance. It is also clear that a conservative activist could by proposing, say, voluntary social security be initiating major redistribution, but in a direction favoring the rich rather than the poor. Indeed, Hayes (1978) argues that most redistributive policies benefit the powerful. Some element of this negative redistribution appears in the policies of Presidents Nixon and Ford (Vogler 1977). This is especially true for President Reagan. Therefore redistributive policies appear to contain a directional component that could be studied in future research.

Agenda-Setting

2

PRESIDENTIAL LEADERSHIP FROM PUBLIC STATEMENTS

Agenda-setting is the recognition of a problem of a public nature, thereby requiring governmental action. Chapter 1 showed that such problems generally result from conflict where elements in society seek to convince government of the problem's existence. The term *agenda-setting* as used here is limited to the point where the problem becomes salient to the President—not its origin or the actions required for Presidential awareness of the problem. The focus is only on the Presidentially set portion of the public agenda. Although the term may "imply a single mind deciding what will be on the agenda, establishing priorities and deadlines for actions on agenda items" (Eyestone 1978, 100), agenda-setting is a far more important and complicated process than that.

Nature of Agenda-Setting

Roger Cobb and Charles Elder (1972) have written an important theoretical work on how an issue reaches the public policy agenda. They distinguish between a systemic agenda (which includes all potential issues of salience to the general public) and an institutional agenda (which is the action agenda of more specific and concrete issues upon which policymakers have decided to focus; 1972, 85). It is this latter notion that is concentrated on more directly—the agenda after much of the defining and group conflict has been resolved. This is not to suggest that the institutional (or public) agenda is unambiguous, however, since it is not usually highly structured or well defined. Policymakers seldom are faced with a clearly defined problem; frequently it must be identified, clarified, and ranked in importance with other problems. Although this suggests rational decision making, policymakers often do none of these tasks very well, if at all.

Because issues must compete for inclusion and position on the public policy agenda, those likely to generate substantial opposition may be left off. (An example is civil rights during the first two years of the Kennedy Administration; Shank 1980, Ch. 5.) At the same time, issues stand a greater chance of attaining agenda status if they can expand in scope, intensity, and visibility. These conditions can also increase opposition to the point that the issue will not reach government's agenda. Although there is no guarantee that once an item reaches the public agenda it will stay, issues seldom leave once they gain access (Cobb and Elder 1972, 158-60). Indeed, older items are probably most common and usually receive greater priority (Cobb and Elder 1972, 89). The public policy agenda need not be made up of new items, and when new issues do occur, they frequently are precipitated by crises, as in the call for new safety standards following the mishap at the Three Mile Island nuclear plant. The energy crisis, the Soviet invasion of Afghanistan, and urban rioting are examples of triggering events that prompted renewed emphasis on old issues on the public agenda. Crises may also encourage innovation and early resolution of the policy problem.

Like later policy substages, agenda-building probably reflects the larger environment. The agenda-setting process helps define and refine issues, with the "public agenda [being the] . . . aggregate of individual agendas of everyone in society" (Eyestone 1978, 79). The role of public opinion at this stage is minimal because agenda-setting occurs so early in the process. However, other nongovernmental actors, such as interest groups through political action and political parties through platforms, have influence in developing the public agenda. Redford's (1969, 117) assertion that elections and platforms have little influence on the public agenda suggests that only interest groups among nongovernmental actors have major impact (Light 1982, 93).

Political leadership from the President is crucial in the present definition of agenda-setting. In *Democracy in the Administrative*

State, Emmett Redford discusses how the President can define many policy issues by virtue of his national constituency. This is particularly true for broader issues affecting many interests, what Redford calls macropolitics (1969, 107-23). Through the use of rhetoric, Presidents set an agenda to promote and communicate their policy preferences to those inside and outside government. Such rhetoric is particularly necessary in the intensely conflictual domestic arena where support for policy change is more difficult to obtain (Light 1982). Presidential advocacy is especially likely to occur just before or after a major initiative—before to disseminate information and prepare actors for the proposal and afterward to legitimize or justify what has been proposed. Regardless of when it occurs, advocacy by the President is usually required to inspire the nation toward innovative policies. President John F. Kennedy, for example, appealed with great flourish to patriotism and American know-how in advocating putting a man on the moon before 1970.

An indicator of an issue's position on the public policy agenda can be obtained from Presidential messages. These public documents reflect the culmination of Presidential agenda-building (Cobb and Elder 1972). It is asserted here that much of what appears on the public agenda can be traced to the rhetoric in Presidential statements. Certainly a lot of Presidential rhetoric is simply that (trial balloons are an example), but much of it is also systematically part of the public agenda if the President can persuade other participants that these issues merit governmental attention. This chapter seeks to establish the degree to which Presidential leadership emerges from his rhetoric in setting the public agenda.

Determining Presidential Preferences

Presidential agenda preferences are obtained from the President's written and spoken comments that establish policy interests, goals, and possibly even priorities. In order to obtain direct, systematic measures of such preferences, content analysis of all presidential speeches, press conferences, letters, and other public messages as recorded in the *Public Papers of the Presidents* is used. A valuable book on Presidential agenda-setting by political scientist Paul Light appeared in 1982. Light uses interviews with staff and legislative requests from Presidents' State of the Union messages as sources of their agendas. The present study casts a broader net for the Presidential agenda since policy preferences are obtained from all such public documents. The rationale is that earlier statements may be suggestive of later legislative requests but that specific proposals usually occur after the more general agenda is set.

A precedent exists for using presidential documents to categorize specific statements into broad policy areas (Kessel 1974, 1975).[1] For this study, Presidential utterances on each policy area were located by using key words (such as *civil rights, discrimination,* and *equality*) selected from the extensive index included in the annual editions of the *Public Papers*. The key words utilized appear in the Methodological Appendix.

Several indicators of Presidential attention to a potential agenda issue are used. The first is simply to record how many items (the titles of each public document) in the *Public Papers* fall primarily into each policy area.[2] This counting of each separate document broadly illustrates the President's public issue emphasis. The second and primary measure focuses more directly on the content of specific policy statements contained in the items. A third indicator consists of the Presidential communications made only to Congress, such as veto statements or special messages. All three measures have both advantages and disadvantages, but because legislative communications are so few as not to be distinguished by policy area, the discussion of its properties is relegated to the Methodological Appendix.

The title of each Presidential document (item) usually provides a rough measure of Presidential attention to policy issues. Their brevity (sometimes a few words) allows only the broadest categorization into substantive issue-areas. Because the number of items may relate simply to Presidential style, a measure of Presidential attention to more specific policy areas is needed. In addition, it is necessary to determine policy preferences (issues on which Presidents are supportive or nonsupportive). An examination of policy statements frequently found within the items is therefore incorporated.

A policy statement is defined as any prominent expression of philosophy, attitude, or opinion about policy issues. For an expression to qualify as a policy statement, the President must explicitly encourage, propose, support, or oppose specific actions or behavior and may refer to past, present, or future policy. Overall, a large number of statements by the Presidents under consideration were located that met this criterion. The number of policy statements per year, like number of items, is an indicator of the changing level of Presidential attention.

In addition to measuring Presidential attention, support for particular policy areas is also of concern. Each policy statement was coded as supportive, nonsupportive, or neutral according to a determination of the President's position. Favoring policies sought by civil rights activists and minorities is an example of a supportive position on civil rights. More specifically, support could advocate legislation or litigation directed against segregation or racial discrimination, as well as seeking such remedial tools as busing or stronger enforcement of civil rights statutes. Supportive positions in all areas except crime would favor increased government involvement. Supportive statements on crime policy advocate procedural guarantees for the accused and reduced criminal penalties. Nonsupportive statements favor both increased penalties and funding. A more detailed discussion of these indicators of attention and support in Presidential agenda-setting may be found in the Methodological Appendix.

BROADER SUBSTANTIVE AGENDA

Overview

An initial look at Presidential rhetoric can be seen in Figure A-1 in the Appendix, which shows that the yearly number of items (documents) during the thirty-one years from 1945 to 1975 has been gradually increasing. Although a dip occurred in the late 1960s and early 1970s, this upward trend is unmistakable and probably due to increased expectations of Presidential performance. Although it would be too simplistic to equate distributive, regulatory, and redistributive policies with the broad substantive divisions of domestic, economic, and foreign issues, respectively, similarities do exist. Because of the difficulty of categorizing the anticipated huge number of items and policy statements into functional areas, the examination of typologies in this chapter only categorizes the data into broad and narrow substantive areas.[3]

The relative distribution of Presidential items across broad policy areas has remained fairly stable across the thirty years for which data are available (see Figure 2-1). Foreign policy dominated Presidential statements until the Johnson Administration. This dominance is partly attributable to the obligatory nature of many foreign policy events, such as visits by foreign dignitaries. Periods of wartime (Korea in the early 1950s and Vietnam in the late 1960s) require greater Presidential rhetoric in foreign policy.

Economic issues were the least prominent policy area, as shown in Figure 2-1. They grew in the 1940s and 1970s, and if data were available, this trend would probably continue through the present time on the graph. Overall, economic issues were less volatile than either domestic or foreign issues.

Domestic issues seem to vary inversely with foreign issues; an emphasis on one means relatively less attention to the other. This finding lends credence to the cliché that guns come at the expense of butter. In summary, items in public documents have been heavily foreign policy oriented, but domestic and economic rhetoric began to increase by the mid-1970s.

Environmental Conditions

Several variables help to explain why Presidents emphasize rhetoric in one policy area at the expense of others. Examining the data by political party, by selected years, and then by individual Presidents provides decreasing levels of generality and should reveal interesting patterns among policy areas.

Party and Year

The analysis reveals generally increasing Presidential rhetoric by both Democrats and Republicans. More documents occur in years when Democrats are Presidents; indeed, Democrats had 57 percent of all Presidential mesages. But because Democrats were in office 52 percent of the time from 1945 through 1975, little party difference exists in amount of overall rhetoric. Regarding the broad policy areas, Democrats are more vocal on domestic and foreign issues, while the Republicans have a slight edge on economic issues (see Figure 2-2).

Certain years may also be singled out for particular attention. Presidents were assumed to be more active during their first and

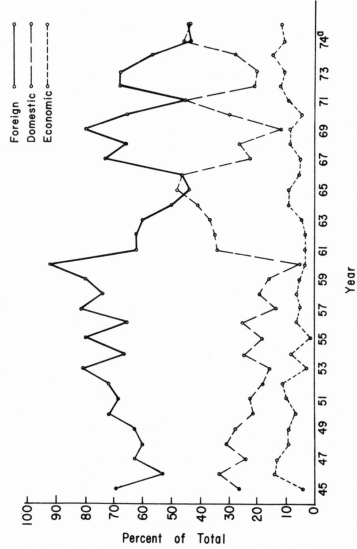

Figure 2-1. Proportion of Items (by Policy Area)

a. Ford

last years in office and less so during reelection years (Light 1982, 41; Kessel 1975, 9). However, despite the final opportunity for historical action and esteem, Presidents actually are least rhetorical during their last year in office and are most vocal during their first (see Figure 2-2). Presidents average seventy-two statements during their last, seventy-four during reelection, and ninety-one during first years in office. In examining specific areas, Presidents are found to be more rhetorical on foreign policy during first and last years, with fewer items in reelection years. This finding validates the frequent observation that foreign policy is seldom controversial and rarely is a factor in Presidential elections. Conversely, domestic and economic issues are emphasized least often during a President's last (nonreelection) year, when the rhetorical focus is much more on foreign policy.

Presidents Individually

Individual Presidents may be compared on the amount of rhetoric overall and in each policy area. Because of the widely differing terms of office, the average number of items per year are provided.[4] Presidents Johnson and Kennedy had the most public documents and Eisenhower and Truman the least (see Figure 2-2). Truman and Eisenhower were also the least rhetorical Presidents in each policy area. Kennedy, squaring with his characterization by some as a "cold warrior" (Donovan 1974, 184; Fairlie 1973), was the most rhetorical of all in foreign policy, despite the presence of war during the other Administrations. Johnson's preferences were in the domestic arena and it is there that he had far more remarks per year than any other President. (See Light 1982 for complementary findings.)

It is well known that Nixon, like Kennedy, was greatly interested in foreign policy. He ranked highest among Republicans in the number of rhetorical statements (see Figure 2-2) but was not as vocal as some might have guessed. Ford evidenced a surprising amount of rhetoric, particularly on domestic and economic policy, the latter due in part to the recession of 1974. Unlike his Republican predecessors, Ford had little personal interest in foreign policy, an area that exhibited increasing legislatively imposed constraints. Ford did give considerable attention (number of items) to foreign policy, however (see Figure 2-2).

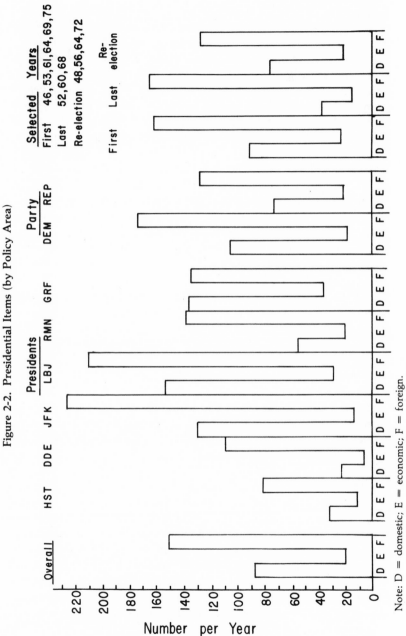

Figure 2-2. Presidential Items (by Policy Area)

Note: D = domestic; E = economic; F = foreign.
Selected years refer to a particular full year in an Administration.

The environmental variables helped to distinguish Presidential emphasis in setting a broad policy agenda. A larger amount of rhetoric by Democrats was not surprising, and domestic issues reflected the biggest differences between the two political parties. Aggregating the data by particular years in office revealed Presidential rhetoric diminishing after the President's first year in office. Analysis of individual Presidents showed an overall increase in rhetoric through Johnson and then a subsequent decline.

NARROWER SUBSTANTIVE AGENDA

Investigation of narrower substantive areas allows more precise study of Presidential agenda preferences. Not only are issues more easily categorized, but explicit policy statements can be used to determine both Presidential attention and support. The content of the policy statements is examined first, then the data are presented both overall and while controlling for environmental conditions (party, selected years in Presidential terms, and Presidents individually).

Content of Domestic Agenda

Which issue-areas have been most salient to recent Presidents? Are civil rights and poverty more important to Presidents than price supports and public works? Are regulatory issues (crime and antitrust) increasing in importance and redistributive areas fading (Light 1982, 85-86)? Which specific subissues are salient? Have these changed over the years?

Price Supports

President Eisenhower proposed decreasing mandatory price supports for certain products, less restrictive acreage controls, and limits on the dollar amount an individual farmer or unit could receive. In a special message on March 16, 1961, Kennedy advocated broadening the support system, and in 1962 he recommended legislation designed to protect farmers who suffer damage from foreign import competition. Johnson also recommended expansion of most support programs (such as rice), but he called for production and marketing limits (*Public Papers*, 1965, 144-45). In a special message to Congress in 1968, he proposed establishing a national food bank to provide a security reserve of food to protect farmers and consumers.

Nixon argued in 1973 that wheat, dairy, feed grain, and cotton allotments were drastically outdated and also sought to end meat import quotas. In a 1974 address before a joint session of Congress, Ford asked for removal of all acreage limits on rice, peanuts, and cotton (*Public Papers*, 1974, 230). He continually, albeit unsuccessfully, sought to get the government out of farming through its storing of surpluses.

Most of Carter's statements dealt with support to sugar producers. He announced an import fee and sought an international sugar agreement but supported subsidies only to cover costs of production, not at the higher profit-making level requested by sugar growers. He also expressed continued approval of price supports for tobacco and opposition to mandatory agricultural price controls. Little change in the agricultural price support agenda was in evidence in the early 1980s. Carter had largely continued the status quo, and Reagan, who was expected to move toward free market conditions, deferred to southern conservative Democrats in continuing support payments for rice and tobacco. This deference was largely a quid pro quo to obtain Democratic support for budget and tax cuts for fiscal 1982 and beyond. Reagan did advocate a payment in kind plan (PIK) early in 1983 to give farmers surplus grain if they agreed not to plant up to half of their acreage. They could either sell the grain or feed it to their live stock, thereby reducing surpluses.

Public Works

Unlike price supports, public works is a much broader distributive issue-area encompassing many subissues, including transportation, parks, and water projects. This discussion of policy content, however, focuses on water only.[5] The primary agenda item under Eisenhower was the construction with Canada of the St. Lawrence Seaway. Although he continued to support the project and touted its successful development, his persistent theme in all water resources was deemphasis on the federal role and maximum participation by state, local, and private interests (see, for example, *Public Papers*, 1955, 18). In 1958 Eisenhower deferred a number of water projects due to the economy and from 1958 through 1960 spoke of his need to veto several water measures Congress passed. In contrast, Kennedy and Johnson stepped up federal help to state and local governments for public works, particularly in depressed economic areas. Kennedy advocated saline water conversion, and Johnson pushed a Water Resources Planning Act to assess future water needs. Johnson advocated increased flood protection and announced construction on two-hundred water projects, with seventy more scheduled (*Public Papers*, 1964, 1083-84, 1566).

Nixon proposed full funding in fiscal 1972 of $327 million (and also in 1974) for the Land and Water Conservation Fund, a program begun by Johnson. He also advocated watershed and flood control development. Ford was much less supportive of water projects. Although he expressed strong support for the controversial Tennessee-Tombigbee project in 1975 and 1976, he made numerous recissions, deferrals, and even vetoes of public works programs.

Carter's primary emphasis in public works policy was to eliminate what he perceived as waste and inefficiency in water projects. He believed such pork barrel projects would be reduced if states were required to share in their financing. In one special message to Congress (2/21/77) he tried to terminate nineteen water projects, and in another during 1978 he sought a more comprehensive federal water policy. Carter will long be remembered for his only partially successful efforts to kill several water projects, but he also pushed for renewed emphasis on hydroelectric power development. Although by 1980 hydroelectric power was the third largest power source (after coal and gas), Reagan sought to curtail the program sharply (*National Journal*, 5/30/81, 977). Reagan even proposed user fees from boat and barge owners, operators of private aircraft, and increased premiums for federal flood insurance. All told, he began his Administration with a massive deemphasis on the federal role in public works.

Crime

Prior to the Johnson Administration, no policy statements (and only three items on crime by Eisenhower) appeared in the *Public Papers*. From 1967 until 1972, however, crime became an increasingly salient issue on the Presidential agenda. Civil disobedience was a major subissue in the late Johnson and early Nixon Administrations. The thrust of the Johnson statements (in two State of the Union addresses and several special messages to Congress on crime) emphasized aiding state and local governments, gun control, and enforcement of drug laws.

The focus on drug abuse intensified throughout the 1970s, as did new attention to organized crime. In numerous special messages, Nixon sought allout war on crime, frequently with little concern for the accused. In his efforts to get criminals out of circulation, Nixon advocated mandatory minimum sentences, fewer pretrial releases for multiple offenders, generally heavier penalties, and selection of judges who were strict on crime (Shull and Heck 1980). This emphasis was continued by Ford, who, in a 1975 special message to Congress on crime, sought to reduce plea bargaining and trial delays and also to restrict the sale of cheap handguns. Carter's moderate positions on juvenile crime, decriminalization of marijuana, and limiting handguns were modified when Ronald Reagan entered the White House. Reagan's opposition to gun control persists, despite an assassination attempt on his life in March 1981.

Antitrust

Presidents except Ford and Reagan strongly supported government efforts to eliminate monopolies and enforce the existing antitrust laws. Only Eisenhower, Ford, and Carter had much to say about this policy area, with the former advocating greater funding to increase the Justice Department's review capability.[6] Vigorous enforcement was called for throughout the 1950s in budget messages and in the Economic Report to Congress. Ford began by creating a strong antitrust record. He recommended action against American Telephone and Telegraph Co. and prosecution of violators of the Sherman Anti-Trust Act. But during the 1976 election campaign, Ford took quite conservative positions on antitrust. Although Carter brought litigation against antitrust violators, he was also a strong supporter of government deregulation. Thus, he took a typically liberal position on the few general antitrust issues like price fixing but a more characteristically conservative position on deregulation, expounding the benefits of private enterprise, competition, and free market forces. Carter was proud of his successful efforts to deregulate the airline industry, a topic that pervaded many of his major speeches in 1978 and 1979.

Reagan's deemphasis on regulatory government promised diminishing antitrust activities. Early evidence indicates that Reagan is far more sympathetic to bigness and business mergers (*Newsweek*, 7/6/81, 57-58), and he tried to rid the Federal Trade Commission (FTC) of its antitrust activities (*National Journal*, 5/23/81). Ford and Reagan were the first Presidents to back off vigorous enforcement of antitrust violations.

Civil Rights

Civil rights policy statements varied widely across subissues. Except for a general category that cut across a number of issues, education was the largest category of statements (17 percent of all statements), followed by employment (14 percent) and voting (12 percent). Johnson was not the leader in number of statements on education; fully 65 percent of such statements were made by Nixon. Johnson and Nixon led the Presidents on statements about housing, and Johnson and Eisenhower had the most statements on voting issues. The concept of equal rights for women was supported by every President except Reagan, while the issue of jury discrimination was of expressed concern only to Johnson.

The subissue of civil rights examined here is school desegregation, of increasing concern to each of the Presidents until Carter, when controversy finally began to subside. As early as 1956, Eisenhower threatened court action if schools did not desegregate and also encouraged those threatened by suits not to close. In 1959 Eisenhower sent a major message to Congress recommending school desegregation legislation, and just before leaving office, he extended the life of the Civil Rights Commission to facilitate the desegregation task. Despite these actions, Eisenhower was quite passive in following up desegregation rulings of the courts. With the exception of encouraging the upholding of Supreme Court rulings in 1963, Kennedy did surprisingly little in the civil rights area (Shank 1980, Ch. 5). In 1966 Johnson established the White House Conference on Civil Rights, and for the first time he sought additional funds through the Elementary and Secondary Education Act to deal with the issue of de facto segregation.

Nixon made numerous speeches opposing court-ordered busing and government efforts in de facto segregation cases. He was willing to encourage compliance but with minimum disruption and even using federal funds to soften the blow. Nixon believed busing was harmful to education, and in 1972 he sought a one-year moratorium on busing orders. Ford was even more adamantly opposed to busing (7 statements, with 108 lines solely on this topic in 1975 alone). Like Nixon, he supported federal aid to school districts undergoing desegregation.

The single statement under Carter on October 16, 1979, vowed to minimize mandatory busing but uphold the law. Despite his deep southern heritage, Carter seemed to have persuaded blacks that he was genuinely committed to the cause of civil rights. Notwithstanding the reduced urgency of a civil rights agenda after the mid-1960s, his dedication to racial equality continued. Carter, however, probably will be remembered even more for his international human rights efforts in foreign policy. His views were deeply rooted in his religious convictions, but his good intentions were difficult to follow through in practice. As in so many other policy areas, Carter was not able to exert consistent, determined leadership when realities conflicted with principles. The early 1980s under Reagan seem likely to return to the benign neglect of the early 1970s. Although Reagan's rhetoric generally remained supportive, his subsequent actions clearly reduced the federal role in civil rights (LeLoup and Shull 1982).

Poverty

The poverty area reflects a considerable broadening of issues across time. Unemployment compensation was the only subissue in 1953, but a multitude of other issues found their way to the Presidential agenda by the 1970s. Many new items were placed on the public agenda by Kennedy: youth employment, general federal assistance to public education, and jobs development. Although many of his agenda items were Kennedy holdovers, Johnson quickly placed his stamp on them in his declaration of war on poverty, his top priority (Light 1982, 70). The expansion of the Vietnam war did not dampen Johnson's enthusiasm for poverty programs, since even more new agenda items (JOBS program, aid to Indians, various health proposals) appeared as he left office.

Nixon's family assistance plan was an amazingly liberal program wrapped in a conservative package (*National Journal*, 11/18/77, 54). The emphasis, however, was consistently on job training and work incentives. Nixon bitterly felt the need to reform the existing system "where going on welfare is more profitable than going to work" (*Public Papers*, 9/9/71, 943). Throughout his Administration, Nixon pushed unsuccessfully for what he considered to be welfare reform but with firm work requirements. Ford vetoed 1975 amendments to the Child Nutrition Act, opposed federally funded day care centers for the nonpoor, and pushed for cuts in the food stamp program, all in the name of reserving aid only to the truly needy.

The Carter Administration signaled a return to greater concern for the disadvantaged, although most of Carter's statements dealt with some aspect of employment. He advocated national health insurance covering sixteen million Americans and all children during their first year of life. He also pushed for cash payments instead of food stamps and a job-oriented program in an effort at comprehensive welfare reform. These reforms never seemed to rank high enough in his priorities to receive serious consideration on the poverty agenda. Reagan advocated the most massive cuts in history in what he considered wasteful giveaway programs, such as food stamps, school lunches, and a too high minimum wage for teenagers. Like his Republican predecessors, he too wanted to make certain that federal poverty funds were supplied only to those most in need.

Overview of Substantive Areas

The data reveal considerable diversity across Presidents and policy areas. Public works and the two redistributive areas of poverty and civil rights elicited far more attention from Presidents overall than did price supports and the regulatory areas of crime and antitrust.[7] Perhaps because of its controversial nature, poverty received by far the most attention (averaging thirty-one statements per year, which accounts for about 39 percent of the policy statements of all six areas). Antitrust was hardly salient at all to Presidents until Ford, and generated the least attention of contemporary Presidents (see Figure 2-3).

When Presidents did make substantive policy statements, they tended overwhelmingly to take supportive positions (69 percent of all policy statements).[8] Presumably Presidents believe that strong supportive advocacy is necessary to have their preferences recognized. By far the most supportive Presidential preferences (88 percent) were expressed on civil rights issues. Two other policy areas (poverty and public works) also were supported strongly (see Figure 2-4). Presidents proved least supportive on the crime issue-area (only 9 percent supportive). Recall that a supportive position on crime, unlike the other policy areas, is against increased governmental involvement but protective of the rights of the accused.

Environmental Conditions

The same environmental variables covered under broader policy areas should also provide useful distinctions across narrower substantive areas of public policy. Political party, selected years, and individual Presidents again serve as controls in assessing similarities and differences in Presidential agenda-setting across the six policy areas. (See Shull 1983a for standard deviations.)

Party

Party affiliation of the President is a useful variable for discriminating Presidential agendas. As expected, Democrats are more vocal than Republicans (104 versus 63 policy statements per year). The exception is crime, where Republicans have slightly more statements on a yearly basis. Greater Republican rhetoric appeared on crime, despite the fact that Eisenhower made not a single substantive remark on the issue-area during his entire eight years in office. Crime became increasingly salient, however, especially to Nixon and Ford (see Figure 2-3). Although Nixon made no policy statements on antitrust, the issue-area received considerable attention from Eisenhower and particularly Ford.

Somewhat surprising was the inordinate attention Carter gave to antitrust (67 percent of all Presidents' statements), frequently extolling the virtues of free enterprise and competition. The considerable rhetoric on price supports under Eisenhower decreased for his successors. Civil rights had surprisingly little salience for Kennedy early in his Administration, while for Johnson, the issue-area began to lose some of its enormous salience after the first year or two.[9] Yet it was only on the two redistributive areas where Democratic rhetoric far outdistanced that of Republican Presidents. Increases in Presidential rhetoric on poverty generally can be attributed to Democrats (Figure 2-3).

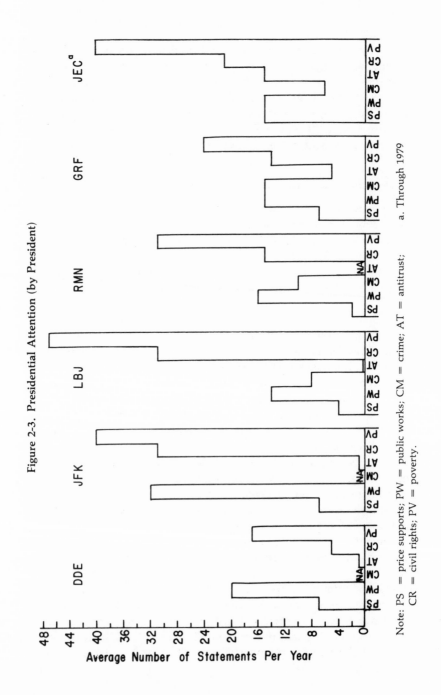

Figure 2-3. Presidential Attention (by President)

Note: PS = price supports; PW = public works; CM = crime; AT = antitrust;
CR = civil rights; PV = poverty.

a. Through 1979

46

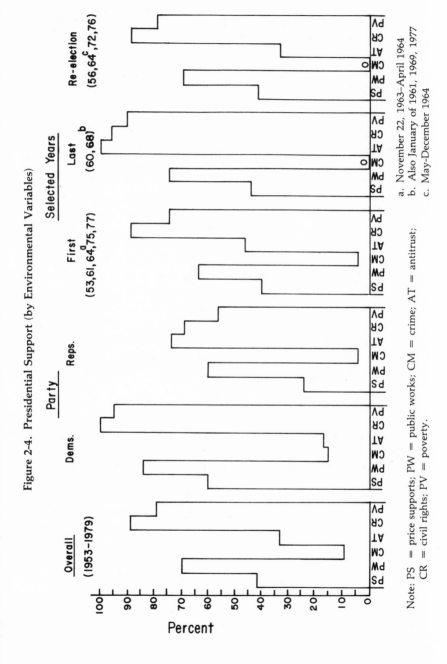

Figure 2-4. Presidential Support (by Environmental Variables)

Note: PS = price supports; PW = public works; CM = crime; AT = antitrust;
CR = civil rights; PV = poverty.

a. November 22, 1963–April 1964
b. Also January of 1961, 1969, 1977
c. May-December 1964

47

While Democrats sometimes said little more, they took much more supportive positions on each issue-area except antitrust, where Carter is the anomaly (see Figure 2-4). Eisenhower made not a single supportive statement on public works during his second term. The mean Democratic support score was 84 percent versus 52 percent for Republicans on all issues. Kennedy and Johnson gave 100 percent support to civil rights and antitrust, with public works and poverty only slightly behind. Johnson was the first of the five Presidents to make a policy statement on crime, and even his seemingly conservative stands on crime (20 percent supportive) must be considered as supportive relative to Republicans and Carter (see Figure 2-5). Unlike his Republican successors, Johnson generally combined his calls for policies aimed at fighting crime with reminders that the rights of defendants should not be sacrificed.

As activist Republicans, Nixon and Ford made more policy statements on a yearly basis than did the passive Eisenhower (see Figure 2-3). After 1971, Nixon's rhetoric declined in all policy areas. Ford made a surprisingly large number of policy statements during his brief period in office, and he was the least or next least supportive President on all policy areas (see Figure 2-5). His 0 percent support on crime is illustrative of his conservatism, as are his positions on civil rights and poverty, particularly in contrast to the more reticent and far more supportive Eisenhower. Carter was the most rhetorical President of all, averaging 112 statements per year (see Figure 2-3). He was also, by far, the least supportive Democrat (see Figure 2-5).

In short, considerable party differences appear on each of the six policy areas, but, surprisingly, partisanship was least on crime, a regulatory policy area that was expected to be highly partisan. Due to Carter's activism, the other regulatory area, antitrust, was most partisan. Although Republican Presidents differed 31 percentage points from Democrats on civil rights, it proved to be a less partisan issue-area than price supports and poverty (see Figure 2-4).

Year

What policy areas do Presidents emphasize at different points in their administration? Considerable divergence is revealed in Figure 2-4, suggesting that these selected years are highly salient. This finding is particularly true for crime and antitrust, where support

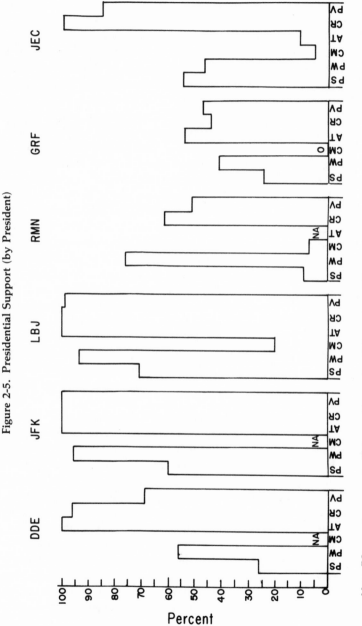

Figure 2-5. Presidential Support (by President)

Note: PS = price supports; PW = public works; CM = crime; AT = antitrust;
CR = civil rights; PV = poverty.

was lower and higher, respectively, than average support for all years. First year in office usually was not as volatile as last or reelection years. Support was least for the two distributive areas and poverty during Presidents' first years. Although crime policy was supported more during first year than during the other designated years, Presidential support was still less than average support for all years.

More distinct patterns emerge for last year in office, where support was greatest for every policy area but crime. This finding was especially true for antitrust and the two redistributive areas (civil rights and poverty), where support was much higher than during other designated years. Presidential support was particularly low for the emotional policies, crime and civil rights, during reelection years. Antitrust also obtained least support from Presidents during reelection. As expected, Presidents emphasize some issues more as they are preparing to leave office than when first entering the Presidency or when running for reelection. The cynic would suggest that Presidents are willing to take unpopular positions only when their job security is not threatened, and only then will they emphasize an ideological stand for their legacy.

Presidents Individually

Throughout this chapter, Presidential attention (number of policy statements) has been used as an indicator of the issues that mattered to each President. A case could be made that attention is only one component of salience. Support toward issues (Figure 2-5) is also important, since Presidential attention, may simply reflect public demands and expectations. But the percentage of such support might not indicate the intensity of a President's preferences on an issue either, and a better indicator of salience was sought. The measure of intensity (or consistency) of Presidential preferences is calculated as the absolute value of the difference between each President's support score on each issue and perfect neutrality (50 percent support). Thus, we can compare the intensity of Presidential preferences across issue-areas. The data in Table 2-1 compare Presidents; the higher the score, the more consistent or intense the position.

The Nixon case offers the best illustration of the potential utility of such a measure of intensity. Nixon made more policy statements

Table 2-1. Intensity of Presidential Preferences

	Price Supports	Public Works	Crime	Anti trust	Civil Rights	Poverty
Eisenhower	23	7	––	50	47	18
Kennedy	10	46	––	50	50	50
Johnson	21	43	24	50	50	48
Nixon	41	26	42	––	12	1
Ford	26	9	50	8	7	3
Carter	4	4	45	39	48	34

Note: Each entry represents the difference between the President's support score on that issue and perfect neutrality (50 percent score). The higher the score, the more extreme the position; 50 = maximum intensity, 0 = minimum intensity; based on Figure 2-5.

about civil rights than about crime. Yet because of his higher intensity score on crime, that was the issue about which he probably was most concerned. These data on deviation from neutrality for each President suggest that Nixon did have more intense feelings about crime than about civil rights, despite the greater number of statements devoted to the latter issue-area. The same could be said of Ford, for it seems that crime was the only one of the six areas about which he cared deeply. Public works also offers an interesting contrast: high salience for the "master politician" Johnson and low salience for the "nonpoliticians" Eisenhower and Carter.

As for the expectation that Presidents whose attention to certain issues was highest would take the most intense stands for or against such issues, it can be said with confidence that the Presidents who made the most statements on civil rights and poverty (the three Democrats) had high support in their statements and in these statements took more intense positions than any other Presidents studied.[10] Kennedy and Johnson evidently felt deeply about all issue-areas except price supports and crime, two policy areas that were of much greater salience to Republican Presidents. Carter again contrasts with other Democrats: greater intensity on crime but less on the two distributive areas (price supports and public works).

Because agenda-setting occurs early in the policy process, Presidents define much of the public agenda. A lot of what they advocate has its origins from other sources, both governmental and nongovernmental. The Presidential agenda was measured by levels of Presidential attention and support, as expressed in their public speeches, letters, and other communications. Attention is tapped by number of policy statements, while support seeks to ascertain the President's preferences through the level and intensity expressed in policy statements. Although statements frequently are general and rather vague, they set broad brush strokes of preference and relative issue salience. With some leveling off in the 1970s, Presidential rhetoric has grown in this media age of increased expectations of Presidential performance.

Classification of the data into issue-areas helps to discern the Presidential agenda more clearly. Although foreign policy constituted the largest number of Presidential documents, a decline in its importance relative to domestic issues has occurred since the mid-1940s, possibly due to cooling of the Cold War. Economic items were fairly stable during this period, gaining stature in the 1970s comparable to their prominence during the late 1940s. More specific substantive issues also changed over time. Decreasing in both attention and support until the Carter era were distributive (price supports and public works) and redistributive (civil rights and poverty) issues. The regulatory area has become more prominent.

Presidential policy statements were differentiated according to such environmental conditions as individual Presidents, their political party affiliation, and selected years in their terms of office. Considerable differences among Presidents were observed; Truman and Eisenhower were least rhetorical, and Carter was most willing on a yearly basis to voice policy positions. Presidents also differed with respect to issue salience: Eisenhower, antitrust and civil rights; Kennedy, all but price supports; Johnson, all but crime; Nixon and Ford, only crime; and Carter, all but price supports and public works. Kennedy was the most liberal and Ford the most conservative on all issues but price supports and antitrust. Carter was by far the least supportive President on the latter, due to the emerging subissue of deregulation.

Political party distinguished Presidential rhetoric by policy area. Democrats were more supportive overall and on each broad policy issue. They emphasized foreign and domestic policies and redistributive issues like civil rights and poverty. Republicans, more than Democrats, focused on economic and regulatory issues. On the narrower issue-areas, Democrats generally were also more rhetorical and far more supportive.

Presidents generally were most vocal during their first year and least vocal during their last (nonelection) year in office. Their last year focused more on foreign policy, which was not emphasized as much during reelection years, perhaps because elections seldom turn on questions of foreign policy. Presidents downplay controversial redistributive policy during first and reelection years but give attention and support to them as they are about to leave office (last year).

Presidents advocate an agenda to assert their policy preferences and to establish their leadership and position for posterity. They must do so also to encourage political support for these preferences, support that will be seen as increasingly difficult to obtain on redistributive issues in the domestic policy arena. We find that Presidents giving the most attention to issues also tend to take more extreme stands for or against them. Agenda emphasis, then, seems conditioned by party and year and such environmental factors as personal involvement and interest by the President, interest group strength, bargaining, the popularity of an issue, crises, and the agenda's sheer staying power. Generally, leadership in agenda-setting seems quite possible for the President so inclined.

A recent case study on mental retardation under the Kennedy Administration provides a fitting conclusion to this chapter (Berkowitz 1980). It shows how Kennedy was able to put the issue on the agenda; he could define the problem but not effect the solution. As much as any other President, Kennedy illustrates the difficulty Presidents face in seeing that their preferences, as expressed in agenda-setting, prevail in subsequent stages of policy formation. Agenda-setting suggests that it is important to try, but initiation, modification, and adoption will reveal how hard it is for Presidents to obtain their domestic policy goals.

NOTES

1. Kessel (1974) determined policy areas objectively through factor analysis, while the policy areas utilized here were identified subjectively through key words and a priori decisions.

2. A "List of Items" appears at the beginning of *Public Papers of the Presidents of the United States* through 1976. They are really the titles of the particular Presidential written or oral message but are at least a sentence long and often provide enough basis for the categorization without having to examine the text of the document itself. Spot checking suggested that the sentence accurately describes the broad context of the statement. I recognize that the number of items may reveal as much about trends in public relations as about policy formation. Certainly there are limits to relying strictly upon the title of such public documents.

3. Although it is recognized that foreign, domestic, and economic issues are not mutually exclusive, for present purposes, items were classified as follows: foreign: national security, diplomacy, defense, military, war, Departments of Defense and State, foreign aid and trade; domestic: all domestic departments but treasury, veterans, local disasters, civil rights;

economic: taxation, budget, treasury, Office of Management and Budget, Council of Economic Advisers, inflation, recession, unemployment. A large number of items were not ascertainable. Those that were not possible to categorize by title alone were deleted, as were those that could have been included in more than one area. Examples of items not classified by policy area include the following: unimportant remarks, toasts and eulogies, elections, civil service, appointments and resignations, national emergencies, and more than one remark upon arrival or departure from a particular foreign country. Only items meeting the above conditions are included in this chapter. Figure A-1 in the Appendix contains all items.

4. The number of years for which data are available are as follows: Truman, eight for items only; Eisenhower, eight; Kennedy, three; Johnson, five; Nixon, five and one-half; Ford, two and one-half; Carter, three for statements only.

5. Interested readers may write to me for summaries of Presidential policy statements on other subissues in these six policy areas.

6. Obviously, antitrust is more complex than the discussion suggests at the subpresidential level. Besides, the President could have an effect on antitrust outside his public statements by a certain appointment or simply by a quiet word to the Attorney General.

7. The analysis in this section and part of the one that follows is drawn from Shull 1983a.

8. A few statements—particularly Nixon's statements on civil rights, Eisenhower's and Ford's on poverty, and Johnson's and Carter's on crime—appear to be mixed, expressing both supportive and nonsupportive positions within a single statement. Read in context, such statements are revealed as largely nonsupportive in thrust and are so classified for purposes of this study. By categorizing even neutral statements as nonsupportive, there is greater assurance that the supportive category is relatively pure.

9. While Johnson's civil rights positions invariably were supportive, his attention to the area (as measured by number of lines) decreased in each successive year from 1964.

10. Civil rights policy statements were fairly evenly distributed among the types of Presidential messages: budget and economic reports, veto messages, press conferences, and other types of speeches and communications. Given the perceived importance of State of the Union messages (Kessel 1974), it was surprising to find so few substantive statements on civil rights contained in them (5 percent of total). As might be expected, a large proportion of these (63 percent) came from Johnson. Despite his rhetoric, Kennedy (and Eisenhower too) made no statements on civil rights in these highly visible messages.

Initiation

3

PRESIDENTIAL LEADERSHIP
FROM POLICY FORMULATION

If agenda-setting establishes the parameters of the domestic policy arena, initiation is the "development of appropriate and acceptable proposals for resolving or ameliorating public problems" (Anderson 1982, 37). The general rhetoric in the agenda-setting stage favors the more specific initiatives in this second stage. Formulation clarifies Presidential goals, usually in some priority order. Contary to the work of some scholars (such as Light 1982), the position here is that agenda-setting occurs prior to actual program requests. Such specific program requests (policy initiatives) help us to clarify the developing relationship between political actors, in this case Congress and the President. Initiatives and their subsequent disposition tell us a lot about actor strategies, choices, emphases, and power. (These notions, as well as bargaining and conflict, are discussed in subsequent chapters.)

The President plays a greater role in policy initiation today than previously, but Congress is significant too. Other actors are involved directly or indirectly in this process. Many Presidential initiatives (and many legislative ones also) have their genesis in the bureaucracy, which seldom encourages policy innovation. We are also reminded of the infrequency of innovation; most policy builds heavily upon existing programs. Nondecisions and the cutting of existing programs may also be forms of policy initiation. Some Presidents (and Congresses) choose this direction of breaking little new ground, exemplified by the Republican years prior to the Depression of the 1930s. Since that time, all Presidents have been more active: some offering expansionist policies, others holding to the status quo, and still others taking contractive positions. Both *expansion* and *contraction* refer to nonincremental change in government programs.

Presidential Initiation

Policy initiation increasingly is attributable to Presidents. Active-minded Presidents probably are least likely to defer either to Congress or to the permanent bureaucracy in developing policy proposals. When innovation or consolidation does occur, it is usually with changes in partisan control of government and early on in a new Administration. Also, while Democrats are more expansionist and active generally in policy formulation than Republicans, we expect the content of initiatives among individual Presidents to be relatively similar, just as were their agendas. Indeed, most government policies will continue regardless of Presidential preferences.

Presidents initiate policy because they wish to develop their own programs, or at least to prevent less desirable ones, and because they seek an image of leadership and effectiveness. The centralization of legislative clearance has thrust this task (sometimes reluctantly as in the case of Eisenhower) squarely upon the President's shoulders. Presidents have little to say about the initiation of some domestic policy decisions, and they require wide-ranging political support before policy change is possible. One scholar determined that a President will more likely initiate programs if feasible alternatives exist and if he is popular with Congress and the public (Johannes 1972a, 15). Yet even change-minded Presidents do not always initiate policy. President Johnson passed the buck to Congress on a number of issues, including a farm commodity marketing bill, permanent antistrike legislation, and fiscal 1968 budget cuts. Presidents may also shift the initiative to Congress in instances where they wish to delay for information or consensus, to duck the blame, or to encourage Congress to handle the particular issue itself (Johannes 1972b, 407-11).

Congressional Initiation

Despite an increasing reliance on the Executive for policy initiation, Congress can still participate in the process. One observer notes that the "President is often neither the dominant nor the progressive partner in the shaping of domestic policy" (Orfield 1975, 20). A number of studies have challenged the President-preeminent model of policy initiation in the domestic realm. A classic work found that Congress was the dominant partner on twice as many issues from 1880 to 1940, although a trend toward the President during the latter years was observed in the research (Chamberlain 1946). Two writers followed up on this study for the period 1940-67 and found a continued major effort by Congress in policy initiation (Moe and Teel 1970). A similar conclusion for the 1950s and 1960s was drawn by James L. Sundquist (1968).

Most writers would not go so far as to assert that Congress, not the President, is the dominant leader in legislation (Gallagher 1977). Yet its areas of leadership in domestic policy include the issues of air and water pollution, strip-mining, oil price controls, mass transit, land use, employment, banking and commerce, campaign financing, rights of women and minors, crime, economic controls and taxation.[1] Congress also has been chief sponsor of some social programs that reallocate society's resources from the rich to the poor, such as Medicaid.

Assessment

At first glance, it would seem hard to reconcile these divergent views of leadership in domestic policy initiation. Numerous circumstances determine Presidential versus Congressional influence in policy initiation. We stated earlier that nonincremental changes are usually initiated by the President. Clearly Congress has less often been the driving force for change (Ripley and Franklin 1980; Orfield 1975, 262). Congress can substantially influence but does not dominate domestic policy initiation.[2] For that reason, the extent of Presidential leadership in policy initiation becomes our primary focus.

Discovering Presidential Initiatives

This study contends that the Congressional Quarterly box score of initiatives is a useful nonbudgetary measure of Presidential policy preferences. The measure excludes nominations, routine appropriations requests, and proposals by administrative actors other than the President. Also excluded are all but the single most definitive and specific legislative request.[3] While the box score suffers from a number of drawbacks (see Methodological Appendix), it is the best available means of systematically comparing (across time, by policy areas, political parties, and Presidents) the public legislative requests of modern Presidents. Scholars are finding this aggregate measure of what the President proposes to Congress gaining in usefulness for quantitative research.[4]

A rational model of decision making would anticipate that Presidential agenda statements translate into subsequent initiatives in policy formulation. However, legislative initiatives, like budget requests, require more commitment and the making of hard political choices than do mere public statements. Initiatives also address more specific issues than do Presidential statements. Therefore Presidents may not necessarily propose legislation exactly in accord with their agenda. Presidential rhetoric frequently does not refer to legislative proposals, so only an indirect comparison of these two variables is possible. Nevertheless, a positive relationship exists between yearly numbers of items and initiatives ($r = .63$; significant at .001 level). It appears that those Presidents who say the most also propose the most, and presumably the President does try to translate rhetorical statements into acquisitive actions.[5]

Overview of Initiatives

The aggregate number of all types of legislative initiatives made by Presidents from 1947 through 1975 is provided in Figure 3-1. We see a curvilinear pattern in these 6,180 initiatives, increasing through the mid-1960s and then dropping off. Despite the fact that Truman averaged the fewest legislative requests per year, Democrats still proposed more initiatives overall (55.3 percent) than Republicans. Surely ideology has a lot to do with this propensity, especially with the post-1969 decline where two conservative Republicans generally advocated less government and made fewer initiatives than their Democratic predecessors. Contrary to what one might expect, Presidents do not appear to propose more initiatives in their earlier years than during their later years in office.[6]

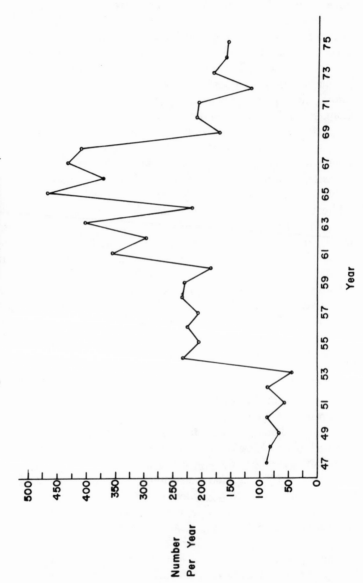

Figure 3-1. Overall Presidential Initiatives

Activity and Government Expansion

Until Reagan, a generally positive association appears between Presidential activism and expansionist policies. Recent Presidents exhibit a wide range of behavior on these variables. We tend to think of Roosevelt and Johnson as the most expansionist Presidents. In the absence of comparable Congressional Quarterly data, bets can safely be placed on Reagan as the activist President most seeking contraction of government. All other Presidents, by being less active than these Presidents, more closely approximate the status quo.

Since the Depression, Presidential initiation of a legislative program has become firmly established. Presidents who are Democrats, liberal in philosophy, with an assertive view of their legislative role, probably will initiate more proposals than those Presidents possessing the opposite characteristics. Support for these contentions appears in Table 3-1, where the number of economic and domestic proposals to Congress by Presidents is presented.[7] Kennedy and Johnson proposed the most domestic initiatives when averaged on a yearly basis. The number of proposals gained substantially each year but tapered off considerably under Nixon and Ford, conservative Republican Presidents.[8] Except for Ford, economic initiatives reveal a similar pattern; that is, more initiatives under Kennedy and Johnson, fewer under Eisenhower and Nixon.

The two most recent Presidents provide an interesting comparison. Carter demonstrated personal assertiveness on some domestic issues, occasionally against the advice of some of his top advisers. He did not propose as many initiatives (see Ripley 1979) as did Roosevelt or Johnson, however, nor was he as personally active. Although Carter's proposals were more expansionist than those of his Republican predecessors, his inability to get most of them off the ground assured that his proposed slogan, "A New Foundation," would not materialize. Surely Reagan is the most active among the contractive Presidents in pursuing his policy preferences, and his activism in a contractive direction through 1982 was profound. During his first year in office, Reagan was quite aggressive as well as politically effective against the disorganized Democrats in Congress in pushing for reductions against long-standing liberal social programs. Contrary to predictions of passivity (Barber

Table 3-1. Presidential Domestic and Economic Policy Initiatives

President	Years in Office (or for which data available)	Other Domestic	Ave. No. per yr.	Economic	Ave. No. per yr.	Total	Ave. No. per yr.
Truman	6[a]	121	20	122	20	243	41
Eisenhower	8	813	102	186	23	999	125
Kennedy	3	717	239	145	48	862	287
Johnson	5	1447	289	140	28	1587	317
Nixon	5.5	625	114	68	12	693	126
Ford	1.5[b]	121	81	45	30	166	111
Average Number per year		3844/29	133	706/29	24	4550/29	157

Source: Shull 1979a, 76.

[a]Data available only for six years (1947-52); based upon slightly different criteria (Congressional Quarterly Almanac 1953, 87).
[b]Data unavailable after 1975.

1980), Reagan exerted forceful, sustained leadership that was in marked contrast to his predecessor, Jimmy Carter, who either could not or would not make peace with members of his own party in Congress. Except for Reagan, then, those Presidents proposing the most policies probably also advocate expansive policies.

Up to this point, we have examined Presidential initiatives overall or broken down into broad domestic and economic issue-areas. These data and the environmental conditions prove more interesting when initiatives are disaggregated by policy area. We now turn to this task.

FUNCTIONAL AREAS

We begin our examination of policy typologies with the Lowi scheme. How discriminating is the typology? Does it discern differences by party, years, and individual President in each of the policy areas? Such differentiation is essential given the enormous complexities of classification (see Appendix), if it is to be useful in examining Presidential-Congressional roles and behavior.

Overview

The proportion of Presidential initiatives broken down into three categories varies considerably over time (see Shull 1983b for trend lines). Figure 3-2 shows that distributive initiatives are proposed most often (42 percent), and regulatory initiatives are proposed least often. Distributive policies were emphasized most in the 1950s and 1960s, but the 1970s have seen some diminution of their appearance. To the extent a trend is observable, redistributive policies show a similar pattern. With the exception of 1958 (possible due to the severe recession in that year) and the mid-1960s, redistributive policies remained an important (if less so than distributive) component of Presidential initiatives. Their relative decline in the 1970s was quite rapid, however. What has taken up the slack is regulatory policy. Very little attention was given to this policy area in the 1950s and early 1960s, but it was the dominant emphasis in the mid-1970s. The predicted rapid growth of regulatory policy relative to others is clearly supported by the data.

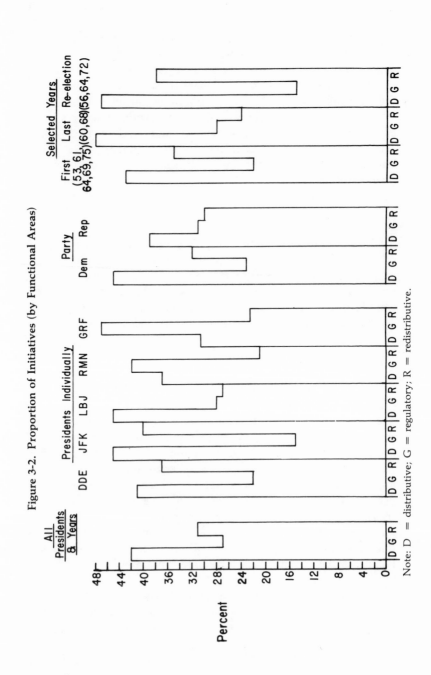

Figure 3-2. Proportion of Initiatives (by Functional Areas)

Note: D = distributive; G = regulatory; R = redistributive.

Environmental Conditions

Party

Figure 3-2 also compares proportions of initiatives by political party, selected years in Presidential terms, and individual Presidents by policy area. Some differences seem evident between the two political parties. Democrats place a bit more emphasis than do Republicans on distributive policies. Probably this is due to the fact the Democratic Presidents had a Democratic majority in Congress. The Democratic strategy has been "inclusive" in that it involves logrolling and providing benefits to a large number of participants (Mayhew 1966, 168), characteristics typifying distributive policy. Certainly Lyndon Johnson effectively used distributive policies to secure Congressional support (Fiorina and Noll 1979; Mayhew 1966).

Republicans focus more than Democrats on regulatory issues (see Figure 3-2), and one might be tempted to conclude that Republicans are more regulation minded, but the nature of the times may also be crucial here. In other words, Ford and Nixon probably emphasized regulatory policy because of its recent importance rather than because of their Republicanism. Contrary to expectation, there is no real party difference in the inclination toward redistributive policies; little influence of party on the rate or level of redistributive initiatives is witnessed. Since the initiatives data are not available beyond 1975, we can only speculate that political climate is more important than party. Democrat Carter, like Republican Eisenhower, would probably rank as close to opposition Presidents as to their own partisan colleagues on policy emphasis of their initiatives.

Year

Presidents are expected to stress redistributive policies in their first year as they are setting forth a broad policy agenda. Their last year or their reelection year, or both, is anticipated to be less regulatory or redistributive and more distributive. Although the differences are not large, there is some support for this expectation in Figure 3-2. Distributive policies are emphasized the most in all designated years. Regulatory policies are not very heavily emphasized during any particular year, and this is especially true during reelection years. While seeking reelection, Presidents encourage popular distributive policies but minimize government regulation. Presidents do shy away from redistributive issues during their last year in office, but not during reelection year as predicted.[9]

Presidents Individually

What appears when we examine initiatives by individual Presidents? These data are also provided in Figure 3-2. Eisenhower often falls between the other two Republicans and the two Democrats in his concerns. Like Kennedy, he focused most on distributive and (surprisingly) on redistributive policies and least on regulatory issues. Johnson's greatest attention was to distributive policies, not redistributive as anticipated. Nixon and Ford concentrated the most on regulatory and least on redistributive issues (see Figure 3-2). This does not seem surprising given their conservative philosophy and also because of the increasing importance of regulatory issues like consumer protection and environmental control during their Administrations.

SUBSTANTIVE AREAS

If functional policy areas differentiate Presidential initiatives, substantive categorizations have even more power to discriminate. In addition to previewing the content of initiatives in these issue-areas, we will examine Presidential proclivity toward policy initiation in each area. Then, because of the large number of initiatives and salience of some issue-areas, we will focus special attention on two subissues: water projects within public works and school desegregation within civil rights.

Content of Policy Initiatives

Price Supports

The Agricultural Adjustment Act of 1933 was the beginning of price supports legislation. Despite the declining attention to agriculture in American politics, price supports have persisted as the most salient farm issue for more than a generation. Overproduction and unstable prices have led to a large array of price support programs, usually dealing with a particular commodity. The lack of unity among farm groups has contributed to the lack of consensus on general agricultural policy and on which commodities are most in need of support. Perhaps due to its past and persistent agricultural nature and political clout, the South continues to receive the greatest share of governmental support. Indeed, most of the important supported commodities—rice, sugar, cotton, tobacco, and peanuts—are produced in the South.

The professed desire of most Presidents to move from supports toward free markets is gradually being realized by the 1980s. A persistent theme of Presidential initiatives, beginning with Eisenhower as early as 1956, has been to reduce allotments and supports. In seeking greater control over the nation's agricultural policies, Presidents from Eisenhower through Johnson often sought to obtain greater discretion to set price support levels through their Secretaries of Agriculture. While federal price supports continue, they have not generated as much attention in recent administrations. Some efforts were made to cut supports for tobacco, sugar, and dairy products in 1981. Reagan was forced to play a careful balancing act: maintaining his budget cuts while not alienating affected farm groups.

Public Works

Because of the large number and diversity of initiatives on public works, the discussion of its substantive content is limited here to water policy. As with agricultural price supports, there is considerable dispersion of responsibility of federal resource policy, principally through the Army Corps of Engineers (rivers and harbors, flood control), the Department of the Interior (reclamation), and the Department of Agriculture (watershed protection). Presidential initiatives on water issues are quite specific, frequently focusing on a particular project. Examples during the Eisenhower years are participation in the St. Lawrence Seaway, and the Niagara Power and Fryingpan-Arkansas projects. Presidents frequently sought either to reduce the tremendous discretion of the Army Corps of Engineers (Maass 1951; Ferejohn 1974) or to reduce the overall level of funding for popular projects. Saline water conversion became a popular topic in the 1960s but began to receive less emphasis by the late 1970s. Attention also began to move away from recreation projects toward flood protection and, particularly, water conservation and preservation.

Efforts by Carter to cut what he considered waste from public works projects in 1978 have been well publicized. Somewhat ironically, Reagan cut far more than Carter but received less criticism (proposing only a $30 million increase for the Army Corps of Engineers in 1982 versus a $250 million increase proposed by Carter). Perhaps the political climate in 1981 was warmer for Reagan, and he spoke largely of delay rather than outright rejection of favored projects.

Crime

Crime is an issue-area of only moderate salience during the years for which initiatives data are available. During the 1950s and McCarthyism, considerable attention was given to internal security questions (for example, spying, sabotage, defense employees); virtually no such Presidential initiatives have appeared since that time. Kennedy tried to get drug laws and a continuation of a 1961 Juvenile Delinquency Act. As in so many other issue-areas, the mid-1960s saw an increased number and variety of Presidential initiatives. For the first time, there were legislative requests to stop organized crime, to halt interstate shipment of firearms, to outlaw wiretapping, and to help fight crime in Washington, D.C. Johnson's most important requests included programs assisting states and communities in their corrections and law enforcement activities. Riot control was an issue that interested both Johnson and Nixon, but Nixon's largest number of crime initiatives were drug related. He also sought stricter penalties in the federal criminal code such as pretrial detention of dangerous criminals and restoring the death penalty for some federal crimes. Ford made some surprisingly liberal initatives (banning certain kinds of handguns, compensating crime victims), but others were of the more conservative variety expected of him (mandatory sentencing, expanding criminal jurisdiction of U.S. magistrates).

Carter seems to have had little interest in crime, but the same cannot be said for Reagan. During his first year, he had Attorney General William French Smith develop sixty recommendations. The proposals went beyond pending Congressional bills in requesting $2 billion in federal funds to help states build new prisons and eliminating a rule that excludes illegally seized evidence from criminal cases. In September 1982, Reagan unveiled additional proposals, most dealing with revisions in criminal law. Reagan advocated greater enforcement, particularly for drug abuse, but actually proposed lower funding levels than had Carter (*National Journal*, 11/13/82, 1936).

Antitrust

The primary purpose of antitrust policy is to maintain competition, but the prevention of unfair or unethical competitive practices, or both, is also important. Although there is disagreement over what constitutes a monopoly, most Presidents have emphasized the desirability of competition. In fact, Republican Presidents of this period actually pushed harder against monopolies than Democrats (Anderson, Brady, and Bullock 1978, 220, 225). Eisenhower sought to increase fines for violators and generally to increase the jurisdiction of the FTC. Although few initiatives were proposed in the 1960s, substantial increases in FTC roles included monitoring honest labeling, fair packaging, consumer credit protection, and proper advertising. (A fascinating example of the FTC's role in formulating cigarette labeling and advertising policy during this period may be seen in Fritschler 1983.)

Nixon, surprisingly, pushed to end the practice of allowing multiple subsidiaries and affiliated corporations to receive undue tax breaks. He even sought in 1971 to increase the effectiveness of the FTC. A partial retreat was made by Ford in advocating that the Interstate Commerce Act allow anticompetitive rate practices in the ailing railroad industry. The Reagan Administration has fostered the view that there is excessive government interference in private business. Accordingly, the FTC has backed away from some cases it sought to prosecute under Carter. Reagan's supporters see nothing wrong with bigness in itself and favor "speaking softly and carrying smaller sticks" (*National Journal*, 4/4/81, 573).

Civil Rights

As with public works, the civil rights policy area includes many subissues, and we focus this discussion on desegregation of public schools. This issue has been one of the most controversial domestic concerns for the last quarter-century, although during much of that time the primary actors were not Presidents but Congress and, especially, the Supreme Court. What each President of the period sought was to ease the burden of desegregation to local government by providing financial assistance.

Presidents Eisenhower through Johnson did request some positive remedies for the school desegregation problem. For example, Eisenhower sought to make it a crime to obstruct court-ordered desegregation. While Kennedy proposed relatively little, both he and Johnson sought legislation allowing the Attorney General to initiate desegregation suits. Johnson also advocated prohibiting interference with attending a public school or college.

Desegregation spawned the extremely contentious issue of mandatory busing during the 1970s. No recent President (not even Carter) has favored such action, and, while Americans were willing to accept desegregation, their opposition to court busing orders increased (Anderson, Brady, and Bullock 1978, 298). In 1981 the Department of Justice proposed to eliminate busing for purposes of desegregating schools. W. B. Reynolds, Assistant Attorney General for Civil Rights, stated, "Forced busing has largely failed to gain public acceptance it needed to work and to enhance educational achievement" (*New Orleans Times Picayune*, 9/21/81, Sec. 1, p. 3). The Reagan Administration opted instead for freedom of choice and for upgrading predominantly black schools. Reagan's actions in civil rights were more conservative than his moderate statements in agenda-setting.

Poverty

Federal housing provides a good example of one relatively salient poverty subissue. The range of housing programs has broadened over the years. Where once public housing was all that was available to the needy, rent supplements, mortgage subsidies, and other programs were developed in the 1960s. Yet the 1950s saw surprisingly liberal Presidential initiatives on housing policy too. Eisenhower pushed for rehabilitation loans, liberalized mortgage terms, and put forth a host of proposals related to urban renewal.[10] There was an effort in 1958 by Eisenhower to reduce federal financial participation to no more than 50 percent net construction costs. Kennedy was active during his first year in office, but housing later took a back seat to employment and education initiatives. Johnson also placed greatest attention to housing during his early years in office. He advocated assistance for the housing problems of domestic farm laborers (1964), a rent supplement program for low-income families, and the Housing and Urban Development Act, which was to be a comprehensive construction and aid program. Nixon and Ford proposed virtually nothing new in the housing area and tried unsuccessfully to consolidate existing programs.

Although Carter supported federal housing programs, the Reagan Administration was not sympathetic to the programs remaining from the Great Society. A Presidential commission on housing in October 1981 recommended an end to federally subsidized housing projects, substituting a food stamp-like rent voucher system instead. The fiscal 1984 budget request included a modified version of this proposal. Reagan also sought to reduce greatly the number of federally subsidized construction units, which had been growing at a rate of 250,000 or more each year until Reagan became President (*New Orleans Times Picayune/States Item*, 10/20/82, Sec. 1, p. 6).

Overview of Substantive Areas

There were 1,774 presidential initiatives to Congress on the six issue-areas from 1953 through 1975, averaging about 77 per year. As expected, several of the policy areas—public works, civil rights, and poverty—show gradually increasing numbers of initiatives through Johnson and then a substantial decrease. The crime issue-area is similar except for the unusually low yearly initiatives by Kennedy. With the two final policy areas, the decrease in yearly emphasis also began early (price supports after Kennedy and anti-trust after Eisenhower; see Figure 3-3). Poverty retains its importance (but price supports, crime, and antitrust are lesser proportions of the Presidents' initiatives). This was also true at the agenda-setting stage. However, we find much greater attention to public works (41 percent of total) and much less relative attention to civil rights in Presidential initiatives to Congress (see Figure 3-3) than was the case in agenda-setting.

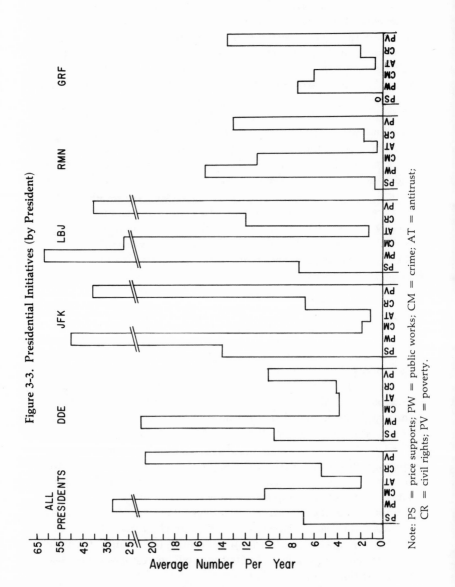

Figure 3-3. Presidential Initiatives (by President)

Note: PS = price supports; PW = public works; CM = crime; AT = antitrust;
CR = civil rights; PV = poverty.

Environmental Conditions

Presidents Individually

Considerable change in the salience of issues occurs over time. It will no doubt surprise some that Eisenhower was more assertive in Presidential initiatives in these six policy areas than either of his two Republican successors. He averaged about fifty-three initiatives a year, which is unexpected given his low activism during his first year in office. Eisenhower had far more requests than any other President on antitrust and was surprisingly attentive to distributive issues, while crime and poverty were not yet as salient in terms of Presidential initiatives (see Figure 3-3).

Kennedy averaged over twice as many initiatives as Eisenhower. He made more requests on a yearly basis than any other President on poverty and, particularly, on price supports. The Kennedy Administration was a high-water mark for subsidized agriculture. At the same time, Kennedy offered by far the fewest initiatives in the crime issue-area.

Following through on his rhetoric, Johnson averaged more initiatives on more policy areas than any other President. In fact, Johnson's requests accounted for nearly 42 percent of the total in the six areas, despite the fact that he was in office only 24 percent of the twenty-three years for which the initiatives data are available. It will surprise no one that Johnson emphasized civil rights much more than other Presidents, but the attention he gave to public works rather than poverty, and crime rather than civil rights, will surprise many observers (see Figure 3-3).

The Nixon and Ford years reveal their greatly reduced domestic programs. Nixon averaged forty-two initiatives per year. Among contemporary Presidents, Nixon placed considerable emphasis on the crime regulatory area but virtually ignored the other regulatory area, antitrust. Civil rights also received fewer initiatives per year under Nixon than any of his counterparts.

The initiatives data are available for only a year and a half of the Ford Administration. That fact compounds another fact: Ford was less inclined to propose initiatives to Congress in these six policy areas than any other recent President (only 29.3 per year). Ford's deemphasis was especially apparent in the distributive areas, price supports and public works (see Figure 3-3), where he seems to have been determined to reduce the federal government's influence.

Although specific initiatives are not available from Congressional Quarterly after 1975, we have some less systematic evidence for Carter and Reagan. Some of Carter's most important requests during his first two years are documented by Ripley (1979). Not many initiatives in the Ripley list deal with the six narrower issue-areas here. Most that do relate to redistributive issues; housing subsidies are of particular interest. Carter's domestic legislative priorities for 1979, according to a liaison aide, included an energy package, hospital cost containment, an urban program, the Department of Education, national health insurance, and fair housing amendments (author's confidential interview). Most of these priorities continued through the end of his term.

Reagan has sought to reduce government's role in virtually every area of domestic policy. What Roosevelt and Johnson sought to build, Reagan has tried to dismantle, and we will witness his success at contraction in subsequent chapters. Reagan's greatest push was in the redistributive area. His budget and program cuts for 1982 and beyond disproportionately affected low-income families and increased substantially the number of people living below the poverty line. (The poverty rate of 14 percent in 1981 was higher than any other year since 1967.) Programs like federally subsidized construction and the Comprehensive Employment and Training Act (CETA) were supported at only about one-third the level Carter had proposed for fiscal 1982. The latter was subsequently eliminated. For fiscal 1984, Reagan proposed cuts in food stamps for the elderly below sixty-five and in meal subsidies for children in institutions (*National Journal*, 10/2/82, 1673).

Party

The fact that Democrats proposed by far the most initiatives (60.8 percent), despite being in office just half the time of Republicans from 1953 through 1975, shows their much greater tendency for action (initiatives) if not rhetoric (agenda-setting). Democrats proposed nearly three times as many initiatives to Congress on a yearly basis and also in every policy area except antitrust (see Figure 3-4). As predicted earlier, Democrats gave less attention

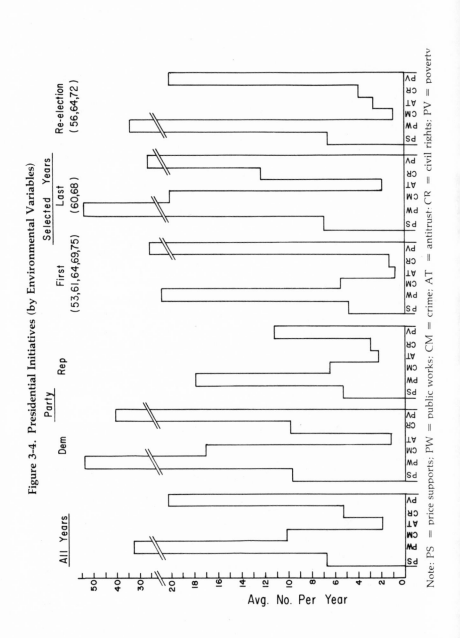

Figure 3-4. Presidential Initiatives (by Environmental Variables)

Note: PS = price supports; PW = public works; CM = crime; AT = antitrust; CR = civil rights; PV = poverty (about 14 percent) to the regulatory area (crime and antitrust) while these issue-areas account for over 17 percent of Republican initiatives among the six policy areas. The greatest partisan differences are in this regulatory area, while the two distributive issue-areas account for just about half of both parties' initiatives. The redistributive issues are more heavily initiated by Democrats, although the party differences are not as great as for crime and antitrust. With the exception of crime, the six issue-areas ranked similarly in importance (percentage of total initiatives) to the two parties. Republicans did spread their attention around more evenly than the Democrats, but they still devote the greatest proportion of their Congressional initiatives to public works and poverty (see Figure 3-4).

Year

Distinguishing among first, last, and reelection years does not work quite as neatly in the analysis of initiatives to Congress as it does for agenda-setting or modification (Chapter 4), where more data points are available. Because relatively few years make up the year-group analysis, we cautiously compare the number of initiatives per year in each category with each of the other year groups and with the average for all years.

Contrary to expectation, Presidents propose fewer initiatives during their first year in office ($\bar{X} = 60.2$) than in reelection years ($\bar{X} = 68.7$) and, particularly, during their last years in office ($\bar{X} = 124.0$). Presidents may be less assertive during their honeymoon period[11] when they are growing used to the office and then find greater freedom to act during their last year in office. However, many of the earlier-year initiatives appear to be broader packages rather than the more specific proposals of later years.

When we break down the data into issue-areas, some interesting patterns emerge. Less notice is taken of all policy areas in the first year, except crime and poverty (see Figure 3-4). All policies are emphasized considerably more during the Presidents' last years in office than during other years. Only antitrust policy received greater attention during reelection years. Policy areas receiving inordinate consideration during Presidents' last years in office were public works, crime, civil rights, and poverty. Presidents do seem to push controversial issues as they are about to leave office. The pattern is not so clear for reelection years, except for deemphasis on crime and poverty initiatives (see Figure 3-4). In short, three policy areas receive much greater attention during Presidents' last year in office: public works, crime, and civil rights. The other three policy areas—price supports, antitrust, and poverty—exhibited the least differences among yearly groupings in the average yearly Presidential initiatives to Congress.

Two Subareas

It is possible to disaggregate some of the data into subissue areas discussed in the content section. No particular reason exists for selecting water projects and school desegregation other than the fact that they are easily identifiable and represent quite different issues for comparison—one within distributive and the other within redistributive policy. It should be quite obvious by now that the two regulatory areas (crime and antitrust) did not offer enough statements (agenda) or initiatives (formulation) to analyze quantitatively subissues within them.

Water Projects

Water projects are perceived as pork barrel by many and are a good example of a classical distributive program where nearly everyone gets a piece of the action. They constitute a rather large subarea of domestic policy in terms of number of initiatives per year (6.5), surpassing our broader antitrust and general civil rights categories and approximating the average number of yearly initiatives for price supports. Water projects constitute 21 percent of the larger public works category and received declining yearly interest after Johnson (see Figure 3-5). Although to a lesser extent than public works, the subissue still divides the two political parties, with Democrats more than twice as likely to initiate them. Also like public works, water policies are emphasized least during first year in office and most during last year in office.

School Desegregation

While school desegregation was a somewhat larger component of its larger issue-area (27 percent), it contained relatively few

Figure 3-5. Presidential Initiatives (by Subissue Areas)

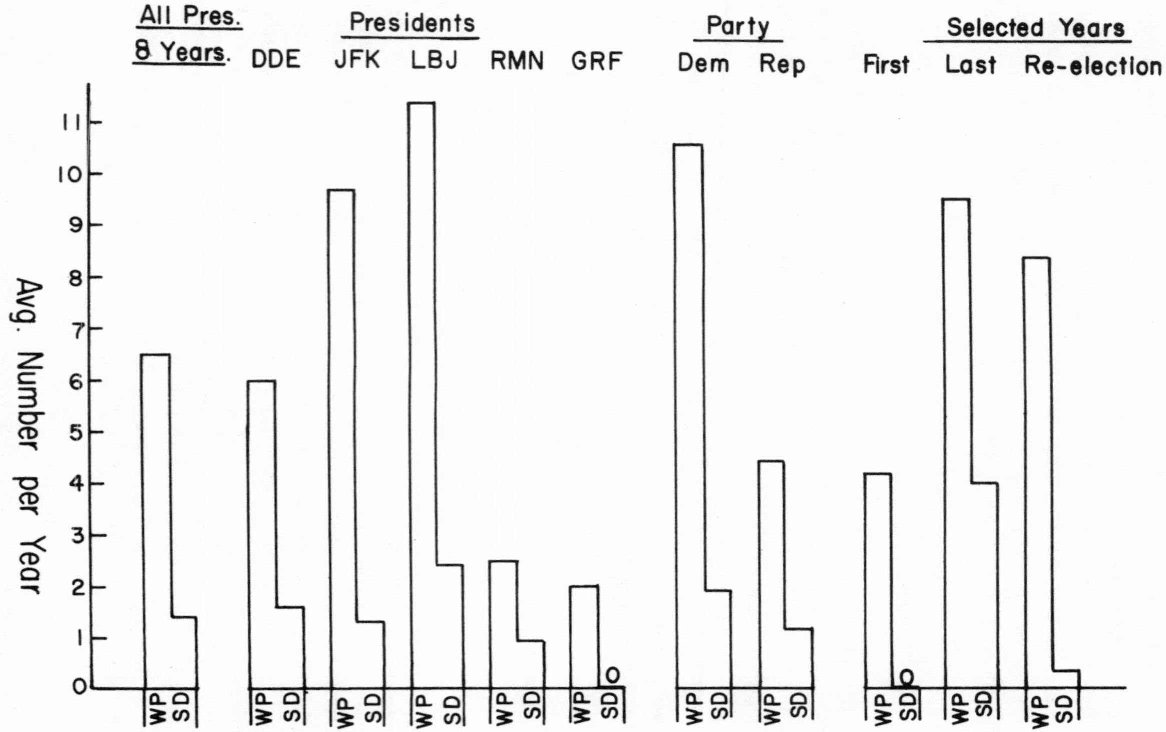

Note: WP = water projects; SD = school desegregation.

initiatives overall, averaging only 1.4 per year. Eisenhower had the most initiatives on an absolute basis (because of its emergence after the Supreme Court *Brown* v. *Board of Education* decision in 1954) and was second only to Johnson on a yearly basis (see Figure 3-5). In contrast to their rhetoric on busing, Nixon proposed few and Ford no initiatives on school desegregation. Primarily because of the large number of Eisenhower initiatives, the party differences are not so great on this subissue as on civil rights as a whole; Democrats initiated only slightly more per year (1.9) than Republicans (1.2). Finally, and caution must be exercised here because of the small numbers, the controversial issue of school desegregation is emphasized only in last year in office, not during first or reelection years (see Figure 3-5).

The President carries out his agenda by formulating legislative initiatives. Agenda statements do not always translate into formulating actions (as with Ford, for example), but a high positive relationship between these two variables was observed overall. The tendency, therefore, is for Presidents who say more to ask for more. Legislative initiatives provide a real opportunity for the President to assert a leadership role. Leadership need not imply innovation; indeed, we saw the persistence of some policy initiatives across many years and Administrations. While Presidents frequently do not actively initiate, such factors as the policy area and the President's interest, ideology, and activism will increase the likelihood that expansive or contractive requests will emerge.

Presidents' initiatives to Congress are obtained from Congressional Quarterly's box score measure, which, despite problems outlined in this and subsequent chapters, allows systematic comparisons of the legislation requested by Presidents across policy areas. The box score is a widely incorporated, useful measure reflecting other elements of Congressional-Presidential behavior as well. The absolute number of initiatives generally increased over time, at least until 1969, after which two conservative Republicans occupied the White House and generally advocated less government. Beyond this most general level of initiatives, their content was divided into functional and substantive policy areas. Differences in the three functional areas of Lowi's typology were revealed, and it appears that regulatory policy is growing at the expense of redistributive policy. Marked differences occurred in substantive and subissue areas.

Variables such as political party, selected years in Presidential terms, and Presidents individually revealed distinctions in both functional and substantive policy areas. The party variable showed that more often than not, the more ideological Democrats requested the most from Congress. Indeed they proposed nearly three times the number of initiatives as Republicans on a yearly basis. However, Democratic Presidents had much less interest in the increasingly salient regulatory area than Republicans. Five of the six substantive issue-areas were emphasized more by Democrats than by Republicans.

The results of the selected year variable were less along expected lines. Presidents do not push more initiatives overall during their first years in office, the honeymoon period. Rather, more legislative requests are made during their last years in office. Redistributive initiatives are requested more during first years, and regulatory issues are emphasized more during reelection years.

Startling differences among the individual Presidents emerged. Eisenhower requested much more from Congress than his reticence in statements (and first-year initiatives) would lead one to predict. While Kennedy requested twice as much legislation on a yearly basis, he had very little interest (least of the five Presidents) in regulatory issues. Johnson had the most overall initiatives and Ford the least on a yearly basis. Unlike Eisenhower and Nixon, Ford was more rhetorical than active. Many of Carter's priorities remained throughout his term of office. Finally, Reagan has attempted great reductions, particularly in redistributive policy.

The legislative requests of Presidents tell us much about actor strategies, emphases, and behavior. Although the focus in this chapter has been almost exclusively on the Presidential role in policy formulation, we recognize that Congress too can initiate policy. As seen in the first part of this chapter, the Presidential leadership role is firmly established, but there are areas where Congress can, and does, take the lead. However, perhaps because of its decentralized, diffuse nature, Congressional initiative most often is reactive to the President. Thus, Congress can take the lead in policy formation but does so primarily through its appraisal of Presidential actions. The extent to which Congress modifies Presidential initiatives and takes a leadership role itself in approving domestic policy initiatives is examined in the next two chapters.

NOTES

1. These areas of Congressional influence in domestic policy initiation have been identified by Sundquist 1968, 535; Gallagher 1977; Jones 1977; Chamberlain 1946; Moe and Teel 1970.

2. Measures of Congress's propensity for policy initiation could include number of Presidential vetoes and overrides, total number of bills enacted, percentage of the Presidents' requests or positions on legislative votes approved, number of reports required of the Executive, Congressional investigations, and subpoena of executive witnesses. Several of these measures are discussed in Chapters 4 and 5.

3. For an example of the rules, see *Congressional Quarterly Almanac,* 1974, 943.

4. See, for example, Wildavsky 1966; LeLoup and Shull 1979a; Spitzer 1979; Shull 1979a; Schwarz and Shaw 1976; Edwards 1980, 13-18; Cohen 1980; Ripley 1979; Shull and LeLoup 1981.

5. The Congressional Quarterly box scores of initiatives are simply calls for legislation, not necessarily actual legislation before Congress. Thus, they show whether the President follows through on his stated agenda preferences but do not assure us that the request was actually introduced in Congress (see Appendix).

6. In a related study, Presidents in each of the four instances for which data are available always submitted more initiatives during their last full year in office than in their first full year (Shull 1979a, 77).

7. Examples of initiatives classified into the two areas included the following: economic: fiscal policy, taxes, the economy, Treasury Department, inflation, budgeting; domestic: general government, domestic agencies, labor, health, crime, public works, consumer protection, transportation, District of Columbia.

8. Since the basis for computing Truman's proposals was different, comparisons including him remain tentative.

9. A related study provided controls for trend on these variables (Shull 1983b). What was observed was a rapid displacement of redistributive policies with regulatory issues (about 10 percent per year). Party differences did hold up on distributive and regulatory policies with trend controlled. Party had little influence on the rate or level of redistributive initiatives with trend controlled, however. Only reelection year among designated years shows any real change in regulatory policy apart from trend, while after controlling for trend, we find the expected likelihood for

Presidents to propose redistributive initiatives during their first year in office.

10. Such urban renewal issues as community development and slum clearance clearly are related to housing but were included in the count of initiatives only if housing was explicitly mentioned in the description of the initiative or if housing was the Congressional Quarterly heading from which the initiative was obtained.

11. Readers may wonder about including 1964 in both first (full) and reelection years. Even if 1964 were deleted from the first year category, the results would have been essentially the same ($\bar{X} = 50.3$ initiatives with the four first years excluding 1964).

Modification 4

CONGRESSIONAL LEADERSHIP FROM APPRAISAL

To this point, the discussion has centered around Presidential leadership in policy formation, but Congress normally has the last word on the scope and specifics of public policy. Although Congress rarely innovates in domestic policy formation, an increasing leadership role has been emerging from its appraisal function. Congress has tended to give the President considerable early latitude but to offer much greater scrutiny later. Thus the primary thesis of this book is that leadership shifts from the President to Congress as the policy process moves from agenda-setting and initiation to modification and adoption.

Congress and the President see the world from divergent perspectives because they are elected at different times and under different circumstances, represent disparate constituencies and issues, and have differing contact with and support from other political actors (Polsby 1976). Presidents frequently are considered cosmopolitan, innovative, and reform-minded, while people attribute the opposite characteristics of parochial, consolidative, and conservative to Congress (Donovan 1974, 57, 70; James 1973, 179). Such stereotyping is obviously oversimplistic; numerous cases can be cited where the reverse characteristics were more applicable (Orfield 1975; Moe and Teel 1970; Sundquist 1981). While the unified nature of the Presidency has given it a larger capacity for leadership in the twentieth century, continued diversity makes Congress the locale for negotiation, compromise, gestation, modification, and rejection of public policy. Certainly most Presidential decisions still require Congressional authorization.

Presidential Resources

The President may exercise a variety of formal and informal modes of leadership over Congress. Formal tools include legislative recommendations (Chapter 3), central clearance of executive programs and budgets, veto of bills (and threats thereof), execution of laws, and the infrequently used power to call special sessions of Congress. A host of informal resources can also be used to buttress those powers: bargaining and persuasion, party leadership and campaign help, patronage (both projects and jobs), public relations through legislative liaison, White House social activities, and the supplying of information. In addition to such prerogatives, the media and the President's ability to influence bureaucratic and public support have also strengthened his power relative to Congress.

Yet for all the President's powers, Congress has corresponding resources. The costs associated with his prerogatives are usually underestimated. There is little a President can do if his program is bogged down in Congress, and he may experience a corresponding diminution of his support elsewhere. Such a situation plagued Carter throughout his Administration. Carter's inability to obtain approval for his energy program affected other proposals and his overall popularity. In contrast, Reagan proved more adept at Congressional relations early in his term, despite Carter's advantage of having both houses of Congress controlled by his party. Presidential resources are relative and changeable depending upon what the President is able to make of them, and leadership opportunities are diminished as Congress asserts its prerogatives.

Congressional Resources

Many of Congress's formal powers have been negative sanctions: resolutions, riders, legislative vetoes, overriding of Presidential vetoes, confirmation of Presidential appointees, oversight of executive implementation, budget controls, and investigations. Recently these resources have been extended and combined with other techniques to strengthen the hand of Congress in its dealings with the President.[1]

Congress has obtained the reputation, justifiably or not, of seldom kicking a President unless he is down. Certainly it made life much more difficult for Republicans Nixon and Ford than was the case during past instances of a partisan divided government. If Congress wants a less powerful President, however, it will have to assume more leadership itself, and not just when the White House is in the hands of the opposition. Critics have charged that Congress is incapable of leadership; that is a characteristic that can come only from a President. Congress does have the resources at least to constrain executive leadership but usually lacks the will to exercise them. In fact, because of increased organizational complexity, Congress may be even less capable of mastering policy events than before. If such mastery is yet possible, it will have to be brought to bear with Presidents who are partisan friends and enemies alike. We shall examine Congress's leadership in this chapter through its assertiveness in modifying and supporting Presidential policy preferences.

DETERMINING CONGRESSIONAL MODIFICATION

Modification refers to whether and how much Congress alters the President's definition of the public agenda. We know that Congress expects the President to set the stage and to initiate proposals, but it is also important to know how much it defers to such leadership. The fact that 80 percent or so of legislation is initiated by the executive branch[2] does not mean that it emerges intact; sometimes legislation bears scant resemblance to the initial Presidential request. In addition to scrutinizing and assessing Presidential initiatives, Congressional modification begins the legitimizing process that culminates in policy adoption (Jones 1977). It should be obvious that the influence has now shifted to Congress. Not only can the President not command Congressional compliance, but he must engage in skillful advocacy techniques if he is to obtain even a portion of his policy preferences. Congress, for example, may alter one policy to gain Presidential support or acquiescence for another. Also, other governmental and nongovernmental actors play their greatest role at this stage, just before policies are formally adopted.

Indicators

Measuring legislative modification of executive policy preferences is an elusive task. There are many avenues for interaction where modification could occur, such as vetoes, oversights, investigations, hearings, amendments, and budget and program requests. More specific indicators include number of hearings or witnesses testifying on legislation, length of time necessary for approval of Presidential proposals, number of countermeasures introduced, number of critical and/or supportive investigations, subpoena of executive witnesses, and number of reports required of the executive. One would have to compare substantive changes in each Presidential proposal with the final legislation approved to determine the exact degree that Presidential proposals are modified. This would be a difficult procedure, as would operationalizing and collecting data for many of the indicators cited.

I sought a direct and fairly tangible measure of Congressional modification of Presidential policy preferences. Congressional Quarterly records the extent to which Presidents take positions on legislative matters (roll call votes). These data have proved useful in measuring Presidential support toward agencies (LeLoup 1975; Shull 1978) and Congress (Shull 1979b). While such position-taking is used to solidify his preferences in the legislative arena, the extent to which Congress actually supports Presidential positions reveals Congress's own assertiveness, deference to Presidential preferences, and executive-legislative policy congruence. During the legislative process, some of these votes and positions are actually changed. But these changes are difficult to get at, so support and related aggregate measures provided here are only surrogates for a perfect measure of legislative modification. Congressional support of the President and the conditions that seem to influence such support have been examined by Jeffrey Cohen (1980), Thomas Hammond and Jane Fraser (1980), and George Edwards III (1980). While many of these votes on which support is based deal with executive-initiated measures, they are now in the legislative arena in frequently revised form. These measures are also fairly representative of all roll calls (Hammond and Fraser 1980, 42).

We use two indicators of Presidential-Congressional interaction: Presidential assertiveness (Presidential positions on Congressional votes) and Congressional support (proportion of times Congress sides with the President's roll call position). Since Presidents take positions on only about 30 percent of recorded votes, these may be issues of importance to them, where they feel it is necessary to take a stand and when their influence could be helpful. Due to the dramatic increase in number of recorded votes, most important measures do come to a roll call vote on the floor. Congressional Quarterly has used the same criteria for approximately thirty years to measure Presidential victories on their legislative roll call positions, so the measure is reliable for time-series analysis. Support occurs when Congress votes yea on a measure the President favors or nay on one he opposes. In addition to assertiveness and support, the amount of conflict engendered by these votes may tap a related component of modification. Conflict is determined by the actual vote split and whether voting is partisan in nature. These indicators should provide useful benchmarks of Presidential inter-action with Congress, as well as make it possible to gauge the Con-gressional role in policy modification.[3]

Modification Overall

The number of positions Presidents take on legislative roll calls has not increased dramatically, despite the huge increases in num-bers of recorded votes in both the House and the Senate. Presidents average about ninety-two positions on legislative votes for each six months they are in office (see Y columns, Figure 4-1). We can compare this number to the proportion of times Presidents took positions (A columns, Figure 4-1). The percentage of times that the President's positions on roll call votes were supported by Congress is also provided in Figure 4-1 (S columns). Congress does vote the way Presidents prefer 73 percent of the time.

Environmental Conditions

Interesting patterns emerge when we study individual Presidents. While Eisenhower took the highest proportion of positions on Con-gressional votes, he was least assertive on a yearly basis. He also received the greatest Congressional support among Republican Presidents, although it was not as high as that obtained by any of the Democratic Presidents. Kennedy, like Eisenhower, also took positions on a large proportion of votes but not so many on a yearly basis, at least compared to Johnson and Carter. Kennedy did receive by far the highest Congressional support of any other Presi-dent. Since this finding does not square with his lack of legislative success in other areas (see LeLoup and Shull 1979b), we can only

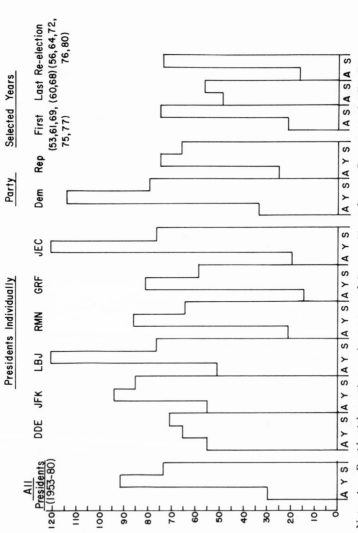

Figure 4-1. Presidential Assertiveness and Congressional Support

Note: A = Presidential assertiveness (percentage of times position taken on Congressional roll calls);
Y = number of Presidential roll call positions for each six months in office, to equalize scale;
S = percentage of times Congress supported Presidential roll call positions.

assume that Kennedy took popular, noncontroversial positions, rarely going against the legislative tide.

Johnson and Carter both took the most positions on a yearly basis, and, ironically, their support from Congress was also identical. Nixon and Ford represented a return to the nonassertive style of Eisenhower and took positions on relatively fewer Congressional votes. This finding concurs with Light's characterization of Johnson as the most assertive and Ford as the least assertive of recent Presidents (1982, 57). Neither Nixon nor Ford received high Congressional support. In fact, Ford had the dubious distinction of being supported on only 58 percent of his legislative positions (see Figure 4-1).

Political party differences also emerge on the propensity for Presidents to take positions on legislative votes. The Democratic Presidents, who always had majority support in both houses of Congress between 1955 and 1980, took positions more frequently and on a higher proportion of Congressional roll calls than did Republicans (see Figure 4-1). As expected, Democratic Presidents' positions were supported more often than those of Republican Presidents, who had a Republican-controlled Congress only once (1953-54).

Finally, selected years also differentiate Presidential assertiveness and Congressional support. Presidents take positions on a higher proportion of roll calls during their last year in office than in other years.[4] Presidents are notably less assertive on legislative votes during reelection years and, unexpectedly, during first years in office (see Figure 4-1). Congress shows greatest predisposition to uphold the President's roll call positions during his honeymoon year than during other years, perhaps because Presidents take fewer positions then. Reelection years were about average, and as a lame duck a President receives very little support from Congress (see Figure 4-1). The lack of support in the last year could be partly attributable to Congressional dislike for Presidential assertiveness.

These findings reveal that Congress goes against the President's wishes about 27 percent of the time. Since assertive Presidents succeed at least as often as nonassertive ones, taking positions is an effective way to exert legislative leadership. We shall see the extent to which this assertiveness engenders support or conflict, or both, in the remainder of the chapter when examining more specific functional and substantive policy areas. Because of differences in data available for the two typologies of policy, we incorporate slightly different indicators.[5]

FUNCTIONAL AREAS

The enormity of the data collection task demands that we concentrate on a subset of data to analyze whether there are differences in Congressional modification across functional policy areas. The data base is derived from Presidential initiatives but incorporates only those initiatives where recorded votes in Congress occurred (see Spitzer 1980). We look at both the numbers of votes and vote split on these roll calls in order to ascertain how much legislative scrutiny and conflict occurs. While the number of votes on such initiatives for the three types of policy (distributive, regulatory, and redistributive) is small enough to make the data management problem feasible, there are still sufficient numbers to provide a basis for analysis without trying to categorize every Congressional roll call, which in recent Congresses has approached fourteen hundred per year.

Overview

Overall there were 1,226 roll calls on Presidential legislative requests from 1954 through 1974, or about fifty-nine votes per year. We had expected the distributive area to be least controversial and the redistributive area to be most controversial simply in terms of numbers (the greater number of votes, the greater the controversy). This finding is confirmed in the first columns presented in Figure 4-2. Votes on distributive initiatives averaged ten per year compared to twenty-eight for redistributive requests. It is important to note that these findings are not simply a function of the number of overall legislative requests; indeed, regulatory requests were the fewest. As we examine several environmental influences, we shall consider another measure of controversy—closeness of the vote—which may be a better indicator of conflict.

Environmental Conditions

Presidents Individually

Figure 4-2 also presents data by functional policy area for the four Presidents who served during this period. Some surprises occur here. There were more votes under Johnson than any other

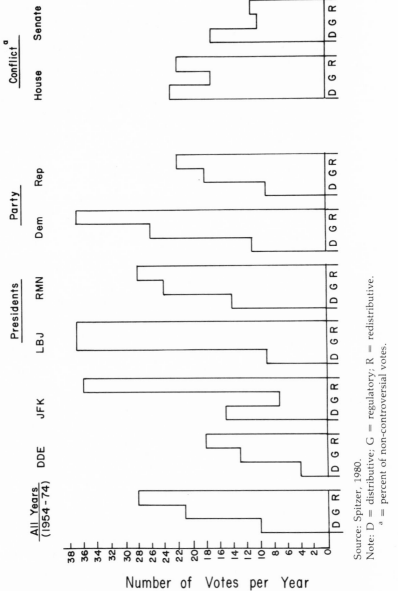

Figure 4-2. Roll Call Votes on Presidential Requests (by Functional Areas)

Source: Spitzer, 1980.

Note: D = distributive; G = regulatory; R = redistributive.
 [a] = percent of non-controversial votes.

President, although he had only slightly more requests that came to a vote on the floor of Congress. Nixon had the next most votes on a yearly basis, yet he had the fewest requests that reached the voting stage. Virtually no differences between the Presidents existed in the proportion of their distributive requests that reached a floor vote. However, Kennedy and Nixon had far more votes on such requests, suggesting greater Congressional conflict for them in the distributive area. Despite the fact that there were fewer regulatory requests than in any other area, the number of votes was substantially greater than for distributive issues. Johnson had the greatest number and Kennedy the least. Johnson also had the most votes on redistributive issues and Eisenhower, by a substantial margin, had the fewest yearly votes on redistributive requests (see Figure 4-2).

Party

Partisan differences were greatest on redistributive and least on distributive issues (Figure 4-2). Although that finding was expected, Democratic Presidents experienced considerably more floor votes on their legislative requests than Republicans (seventy-four to forty-nine on a yearly basis). The fact that both Democratic Presidents had a majority of their party in control of Congress while the Republicans did not suggests that the number of floor votes that exist from Presidential requests is not a very sensitive measure of conflict with Congress. Another measure, the vote split, may prove more useful.

Controversy

If we examine the split of roll calls on Presidents' legislative requests, we find that the distributive issue-area is still the least controversial (see Figure 4-2). Now, however, it is the regulatory area (which also has the fewest votes) that becomes the most controversial issue-area, displacing redistributive policy. Among the four Presidents, Kennedy has the most controversy on all three policy areas. Much of this was due to the strength of the conservative coalition in Congress during his tenure. Somewhat surprisingly, among Presidents, Republican requests generated the least floor conflict: Nixon the least on distributive issues and Eisenhower the least on regulatory and redistributive issues (Spitzer 1980, Tables 7-8). Figure 4-2 also shows that greater controversy occurred in the Senate than in the House on all three policy areas.

Assessment

I believed it impractical to examine all roll call votes for their functional policy type, especially because the number of votes has increased so dramatically. The entire number of votes incorporated for functional areas is fewer than the number in both houses combined in some recent single years. Nevertheless, I believe the data used are sufficient to introduce policy modification for functional policy areas. As with all of the other data, however, I have more confidence in the data, measurement, and interpretation in the substantive rather than the functional policy areas.

SUBSTANTIVE AREAS

Investigation of Congressional modification across substantive areas begins with an overview by policy area of the content of legislative votes on which Presidents take positions. We then examine the data overall and when disaggregated into the environmental variables: Presidents individually, party of the President, and selected years in Presidential terms of office.

Content of Modified Policies

Price Supports

Most of the subissues within price supports remained fairly stable throughout the time period under consideration. Only one President took a position on the issue of tobacco. (Ford opposed terminating supports, although he had supported reductions for most other commodities.) Like tobacco for southern congressmen, dairy supports continued, at the urging of midwestern legislators, to receive strong Congressional support. The milk lobby was continually successful after Eisenhower until late 1981, when Reagan finally persuaded Congress to reduce dairy supports. Wheat, peanuts, sugar, and feed grain supports often proved more controversial in Congress. Kennedy was defeated in his opposition to raising support for feed grains in 1961, and Carter was opposed in his efforts to reduce supports for wheat (1977) and sugar (1978). By 1979 there was a trend toward more general loans and crop insurance in Congressional roll calls rather than price supports for explicit crops.

Public Works

So much activity occurs in the public works policy area that, except for a brief discussion of transportation, the discussion of policy substance is limited to water projects. The first major transportation issue was airport construction. By 1959 mass transit had become an important issue, and federal aid to highways continued to be popular. By 1975 Congress passed federal aid to railroads, which generated much dispute when Congress increased such support over the objections of Presidents Ford (1975) and Carter (1980).

Most of the water-related public works issues in the earlier years were specific projects, but later such projects were deemphasized in favor of omnibus programs in Congressional roll call votes. There were exceptions, however, and such projects as the Dickey-Lincoln power project (1965-80) and the Tennessee-Tombigbee waterway (1956-81) were long-standing and invariably controversial.[6] Presidents were defeated when they tried to cut specific projects or opposed final appropriations for rivers and harbor projects. Unlike Eisenhower, Ford, and Carter, the other three Presidents never took positions in opposition to such projects. Carter's aggressive positions on water development funds (1977), on an inland water barge fuel tax (1978), and on the cutting of eight water projects (1980) embroiled him in controversy.

Crime

The only votes on crime under Eisenhower were during his last year in office. Even those were largely civil rights related rather than traditional crime issues. Kennedy took no positions on the few roll calls in this policy area during his Administration, most of which dealt with capital punishment. Obviously a much wider array of votes on crime occurred subsequently. Congress upheld Johnson's support for penalties for obstructing a federal criminal investigation and for illegal possession of drugs and firearms but did not support his more liberal positions in 1968 in opposition to federal penalties for civil disorders and amendments on an omnibus crime bill. Growing Congressional conservatism in the crime area was encouraged by Nixon. He was nearly always supported in his positions, advocating, for example, an enlarged White House police force and stiffer penalties for drug usage. Such issues as mandatory sentences for committing a felony with a firearm or for drug pushers and allowing the death penalty for skyjackers received considerable support in the early 1970s. Ford, who expressed many policy statements on crime, was not able to interest Congress in this issue-area; few and generally noncontroversial votes appeared. While Carter took only one position on crime in four years, many new issues appeared in legislative votes: child prostitution, penalties for violating nuclear safety standards, and organized crime.

Antitrust

Even more than crime, antitrust roll calls were either many (fifty-six votes in 1976) or, more commonly, absent altogether (none in many years). Even the most rhetorical Presidents (for example, Carter on deregulation) were unable to generate much Congressional enthusiasm for antitrust. After conservative positions in the 1950s, Congress did take more activist positions in the 1960s. It applied antitrust laws to mergers of cooperatives and upheld a 1962 Kennedy-backed measure allowing the Attorney General to demand business records. Antitrust was relaxed somewhat in the early 1970s for such financially ailing industries as newspapers and railroads. Yet, the Senate unanimously passed S. 782 on July 18, 1973, to increase penalties for antitrust violators. The huge number of votes in 1976 were mostly amendments applying to states, such as allowing suits on behalf of their citizens. The few votes under Carter were mostly industry-specific, although the House unanimously upheld Carter's position in 1980 that private antitrust suits were essentially the same as government suits.

Civil Rights

Eisenhower, and perhaps not so surprising by now, Kennedy, took very few positions on civil rights votes. Eisenhower was not particularly consistent. He opposed a ban on discrimination in school facilities built with federal funds but supported allowing the Attorney General to file desegregation suits. In 1960 he was defeated by the House on the former but upheld by the Senate on the latter. (Again, we focus on school desegregation in this discussion of the content of civil rights votes.) During the Kennedy years, one or both houses narrowly passed measures (without his taking any positions) disallowing federal funds for a variety of segregated public accommodations. Unlike Kennedy, Johnson took positions on practically all civil rights votes. The major Civil Rights Act of 1964 (H.R. 7152) and the Voting Rights Act of 1965 (H.R. 6400 S. 1564) passed with his strong endorsement. Johnson was not supported in all of his positions (for example, filing desegregation suits and open housing). School desegregation reemerged as more controversial in the 1970s. Early on, Nixon supported (and was upheld on) the requirement that schools must desegregate to receive federal aid, but as early as 1971 he opposed (as did Congress) using federal funds for busing. He clearly sought to delay the desegregation process. Ironically, Ford took no positions on this issue that had been very salient in his rhetoric. Congress, increasingly, took many and more conservative positions on busing. Both houses refused in 1977 to agree to Carter's support for federal funds for busing, but the House did defeat in 1979 a constitutional amendment opposed by Carter prohibiting busing. Conservative legislative votes continued in 1979-80 opposing busing and racial quotas in education. Reagan took a single position during 1981-82, belatedly supporting an extension of the Voting Rights Act, a position upheld by Congress.

Poverty

Because of the huge array of poverty issues, we concentrate on housing, an issue perhaps of greatest concern in the 1950s. There were votes on this subissue in nearly every year of the Eisenhower Administration. Although the Senate upheld Eisenhower's opposition to low-income housing authorizations in 1957, both houses passed public housing monies over his objection during several votes in 1959 and increased the number of such housing units in 1960. Kennedy was upheld on all of his rather noncontroversial positions on housing, such as support for a measure in 1962 providing housing assistance to the elderly. Under Johnson, the huge array of poverty programs placed housing in a somewhat less urgent category. Rent supplements were debated, however, and Johnson was opposed in his endorsement of them in 1965 and 1966. Although he was also defeated on his opposition to spending cuts for low-income housing (March 29, 1968), Johnson obtained support for a program of home ownership for those with low incomes. The Senate in 1970 opposed Nixon's conservative positions on public housing and extended a 1968 act in this subarea. Both chambers expanded public housing assistance in 1972. Congress also refused to support Ford's opposition to federal loans to unemployed home owners. Increased federal assistance for public housing was passed in 1977 with Carter's support by large margins in both chambers. All of Carter's supportive positions (for example, on housing subsidies for those with low incomes) were upheld by Congress.

Assessment and Measurement

The substance of modified policy in all areas sometimes changes character over a period of time. Certainly a broadening of the issue-areas was observed. Subissues change too, and Presidents bring varied interest and commitment to the six areas. In order to assess Presidential-Congressional relations, we present several measures. We begin with two indicators of Presidential assertiveness: average number and proportion of roll calls per year on which Presidents took a position. The number of roll calls that were also amendments is a measure of conflict, as is the vote split on relevant roll calls. A related dimension of conflict is partisanship, and we examine the proportion of votes where the majority of one party voted against the majority of the other. Finally, we again examine Congressional support (the proportion of times Congress votes in accordance with the Presidents' roll call positions).

Overview

Presidents took positions on 33 percent of all roll calls in the six policy areas, a slightly higher level of assertiveness than for all votes in Congress. Presidents were much more assertive on civil rights (taking positions on 42 percent of roll calls) than on antitrust (only 8 percent of Congressional votes). The other issue-areas clustered between 26 and 38 percent of positions on roll calls. Because the proportion of position-taking declines over time as the number of roll calls increases, we concentrate on the second indicator of Presidential assertiveness. This measure is simply the average number of roll calls per year in office on which the President took a position. Overall, Presidents took an average of twenty-eight positions per year on votes in these six issue-areas.[7] The most positions on a yearly basis were taken on poverty, public works, and civil rights (8.3, 7.0, and 6.5, respectively); very few were taken on the two regulatory areas, crime (1.3) and antitrust (0.3) (see Figure 4-3). This measure of number rather than proportion seems a more discriminating indicator of Presidential assertiveness because it is more constant than proportion of votes.

The several indicators of conflict predictably produce differing results. About seventy-five votes appear for these six issue-areas on a yearly basis, and the greater number by far occur on poverty and public works areas. Overall, approximately 45 percent of the votes on the six issue-areas were also amendments. The greatest proportion of amendments to roll calls appears on civil rights (57 percent of roll calls), and the fewest proportion (34 percent) occurs on antitrust. Although antitrust was not particularly salient to Presidents, it still generated conflict on a third of its votes in Congress. The variance produced by amendments was minimal, however, and because it is similar to the first indicator, we discuss its properties but do not provide the actual data on amendments.

Conflict as measured by vote split on relevant roll calls (see Appendix) is also relatively high on these issue-areas, with 55 percent of the votes in dispute. Figure 4-4 shows that price supports and civil rights were most controversial and crime was the least controversial, with only 27 percent of its roll calls producing conflict in Congress.

The final, quite different indicator of conflict is the extent to which the relevant votes were partisan. Here conflict was less likely to emerge; only 44 percent of the votes produced a party vote split. Price supports, again, was the most partisan (61 percent), but so were antitrust and poverty also quite partisan (52 percent). Only 12 percent of crime votes were of a partisan nature (see Figure 4-5). Thus, crime was least controversial and price supports most controversial on two quite different aspects of legislative conflict.

How much support does the President receive from Congress on these issue-areas? Across all six areas, we find high legislative support of Presidents' positions on votes in Congress (71 percent), just slightly less than for all votes (73 percent). Surprisingly, they receive their greatest support on civil rights (86 percent), an issue-area that was quite conflictual. Even public works, the issue-area supported least often, was upheld by Congress 60 percent of the time (see Figure 4-6). Apparently only a minimal relationship exists among Presidential assertiveness, legislative controversy of the issue-area, and the amount of support Presidents receive from Congress.

Environmental Conditions

Presidents Individually[8]

Five of the six Presidents differed little in the average number of yearly roll calls on which they took positions (Eisenhower was lowest at 20.8 and Nixon was highest of that group with only 23.2). Johnson was by far the most assertive President overall (52.8 positions per year), particularly on redistributive issues of civil rights and poverty, but contrary to assumption, he was also the greatest proponent of crime policy. Kennedy was the most assertive President on agricultural price supports and the least assertive on civil rights. Antitrust policy was promoted most vigorously by Nixon, while Carter strongly pushed public works policy. Eisenhower was neither the most nor the least assertive President on any of the six policy areas.

The greatest conflict occurred on votes under Eisenhower; the least conflict (vote split) occurred on the Ford votes. This startling result is partly a function of the declining conflict overall on these issue-areas since Eisenhower and may also be attributed to the increasing numbers of such votes. Civil rights was the only policy area where Eisenhower's positions were not conflictual; indeed, votes on his civil rights positions were the least contested of all Presidents. Kennedy suffered considerable controversy over his stands on price supports, public works, and civil rights, but his positions on poverty were not particularly contentious. Johnson's viewpoints often stirred up controversy, particularly in crime and poverty areas, where many of his positions called for significant policy change. Nixon and Ford did not generate much debate on legislative votes, particularly on public works, crime, or poverty issues. Civil rights is where their stance was most often attacked. Carter's positions did not elicit much conflict either, with the exception of civil rights, for it was here that he spawned more

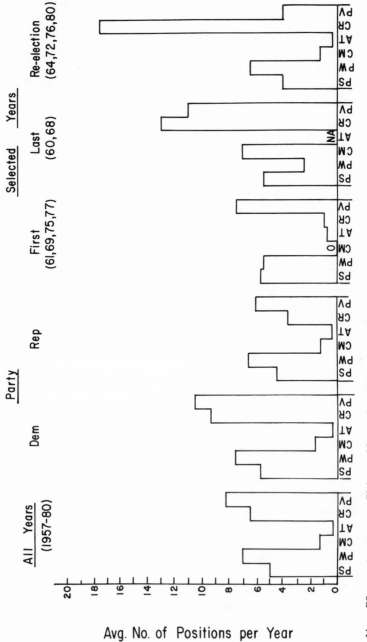

Figure 4-3. Presidential Assertiveness

Note: PS = price supports; PW = public works; CM = crime; AT = antitrust;
CR = civil rights; PV = poverty.

100

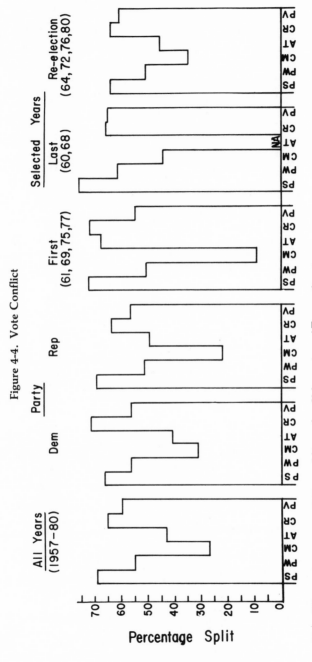

Figure 4-4. Vote Conflict

Note: PS = price supports; PW = public works; CM = crime; AT = antitrust; CR = civil rights; PV = poverty.

101

Figure 4-5. Partisan Vote Split

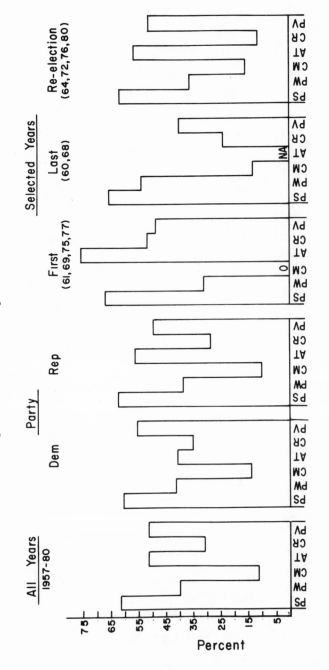

Note: PS = price supports; PW = public works; CM = crime; AT = antitrust;
CR = civil rights; PV = poverty.

102

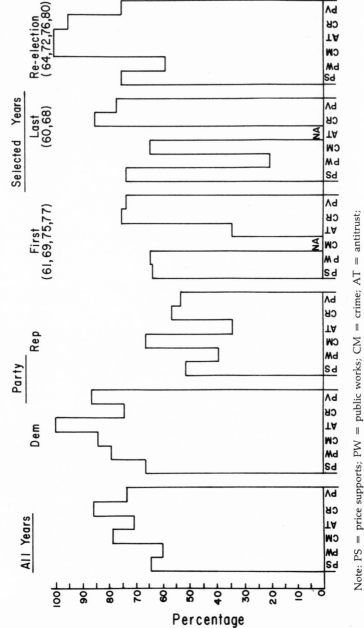

Figure 4-6. Congressional Support

Note: PS = price supports; PW = public works; CM = crime; AT = antitrust;
CR = civil rights; PV = poverty.

103

controversy than any previous President. Reagan avoided controversy by taking one position on civil rights out of forty-five votes during his first two years in office.

The second dimension of conflict, partisanship, also shows a downward trend after the Eisenhower and Kennedy eras. Fewer partisan votes emerged under Nixon than any other President. Eisenhower had the most partisan votes in price supports and poverty but the fewest on crime, antitrust, and civil rights, an unexpected finding. Kennedy had the most partisan votes on three issue-areas: public works, antitrust, and civil rights. A significant drop in number of partisan votes occurred for Johnson and, particularly, Nixon. The Ford positions elicited somewhat more partisan votes, notably on antitrust and crime. In the latter area, he had the largest proportion of partisan votes among the six Presidents. Carter also had relatively few partisan votes, except on the issue of civil rights, where he had a larger proportion (68 percent) than any other President.

The final comparison of Presidents individually is on the Congressional support measure. Kennedy and Johnson received the greatest overall support, Eisenhower and Ford the least. Eisenhower received fairly high levels of backing for price supports and his few crime positions. Kennedy's support was inordinately high on price supports and poverty. Obviously, he did not take many controversial positions on the latter issue-area. Johnson obtained high support for his stance on public works, antitrust, and, particularly, civil rights, where his positions were upheld 98 percent of the time. He was much more likely to be impeded in his stands on crime. In contrast to Johnson, Nixon did quite well on his crime positions, largely because they were more conservative. Nixon received considerably higher support on his positions than the other two Republican Presidents. Ford's support by Congress was extremely low on public works and redistributive issues. Carter obtained unusually low support in general and the least of any other President on price supports. Although he fared nearly as poorly as Ford on civil rights, he received quite strong support for his poverty positions.

Party

Party differences in Presidential assertiveness across the policy areas were considerable when measured by average number of positions on votes per year. Democratic Presidents averaged thirty-five such positions per year versus only twenty-two for Republican Presidents. When we examine the proportion of roll call votes on which Presidents took positions, Democratic Presidents are again found to be more assertive than Republican Presidents. A partial explanation for this phenomenon is the period of time when a President served (that is, Republicans more often in recent years when there are more votes). Party differences appear again when we examine the six issue-areas separately. Democrats take more positions on roll calls in five of the six policy areas. This is particularly the case on the two redistributive issue-areas: civil rights and poverty (see Figure 4-3). Only on antitrust do Republicans match Democrats in assertiveness.

Can the legislative conflict measures also be distinguished by Presidential party? None of the conflict measures differentiates much between Democrats and Republicans when we look at all six issue-areas together. Even when we examine them separately, party differences are not dramatic. Virtually no party differences exist for price supports and poverty, while some differences are evident for other areas, especially crime (see Figure 4-4). Although Congress has been controlled continuously by Democrats between 1954 and 1981, greater conflict (vote splitting) occurs under Democratic Presidents on more policy areas than when Republicans are in the White House.

The related dimension of the partisan nature of such votes was not very discriminating either. The votes on four of the six issue-areas were split more along partisan lines under Democratic than Republican Presidents. The greatest difference between the two parties on this variable was on antitrust, where the preponderance of votes under Republican Presidents was partisan (see Figure 4-5).

Finally, we examine party differences in legislative support of the Presidents' roll call positions. As expected, significant differences emerge. Democrats obtain approval on 81 percent of their positions versus only 51 percent for Republicans. Some of these differences are magnified when we look at the issue-areas individually. Democrats received greater support on each issue-area, with the differences particularly dramatic in public works and antitrust (see Figure 4-6). Much of this greater Democratic support is due to having continuous control of Congress by their partisans during this period.

Year

Differences in assertiveness, conflict, and support are also discernible when particular Presidential years are examined. Presidents averaged nearly twice as many vote positions on these issue-areas during their last year in office (39.0) as in their first year in office (20.5). Reelection years also generated more positions (32.6) than during first years. When we look at the specific issue-areas, Presidents took positions more frequently during the last year on crime and poverty (see Figure 4-3). Presidents took positions more often on civil rights and porkbarrel public works during reelection years. On no issue-area did Presidents more frequently take positions in their first year in office.

As has been the case so far, the conflict measures produced different results. Congress does generate more votes in reelection years than at other times. A higher proportion of roll calls are amendments during reelection and last years than during first year in office. Except for antitrust and civil rights, a considerably higher proportion of votes are controversial (vote split) during the last year than during any other year in Presidents' terms (see Figure 4-4). In reelection years, price supports and civil rights still are much more controversial than, for example, crime, an issue-area that generated even less controversy during Presidents' first years in office.

The relationships are nearly reversed when we examine the partisan split of legislative votes by selected years. Overall, first years are most partisan and last years least partisan, presumably because the President's party mandate weakens. Exceptions and other permutations materialize when looking at the issue-areas individually. Antitrust and civil rights had far higher proportions of party line splits during first years than at other times, yet the opposite was true for public works and crime (see Figure 4-5). Although poverty generated more partisan voting in Congress during reelection years, civil rights was a largely nonpartisan issue-area. Last year in office was distinguished only by rather high party voting on public works issues.

A curious phenomenon emerges when we examine legislative support of the Presidents' roll call positions by selected years. Surprisingly, Presidents obtain by far their greatest support during reelection years and their least support during their honeymoon. This occurs on four of the six issue-areas. Such reelection support is inordinately high for crime, antitrust, and civil rights (see Figure

4-6). Presidents are supported less during their first years on all issue-areas but public works, while this issue-area received only 20 percent support during Presidents' last years in office (see Figure 4-6).

Although domestic policy is largely initiated through the auspices of the Executive, we sought, and expected to find, considerable alteration (modification) of Presidents' positions on legislative votes. Perceived high conflict as measured by split and partisanship of such votes would lead one to predict little support for Presidents' roll call positions by Congress. Although considerable conflict was observed, it had little relationship either to Presidential assertiveness or ultimate Congressional support. Thus, the degree of Presidential assertiveness (advocacy of positions on legislative votes) seems not to affect Congressional resolution of the issue. Despite the inability of these measures to work in concert, the findings, overall and disaggregated, provide useful information and perhaps even some explanations of Presidential-Congressional relations.

The empirical analysis reveals that Presidents take positions on 30 percent of all votes and are supported by Congress nearly three-fourths of the time. Presidents have good reason to be selective in their assertiveness and usually have their way with Congress; high congruence of positions was observed. Presumably, Presidents anticipate legislative reaction. Since they usually are not challenged, Presidents who wish to lead may choose to be more assertive in the future. All three of the Democratic Presidents were both more assertive and obtained greater legislative support than any of the three Republican Presidents. Thus, our earlier speculation that Congress dislikes assertiveness is disconfirmed. Johnson and Carter were the most assertive on a yearly basis, and Eisenhower averaged the fewest positions on legislative votes. Presidents were more assertive overall during their last year in office and least assertive during their reelection year. As expected, Presidents were upheld more during their honeymoon first year but received least support during their last (lame duck) year. Kennedy obtained the highest Congressional support and Ford the least, but he was still supported nearly 60 percent of the time.

Both functional and substantive policy areas distinguished Presidential assertiveness and support. Because of the difficulty of classification, we used a sample of data for functional policy areas.

Useful distinctions between the three types of policy emerged. As expected, distributive issues were less controversial (both on number of votes and vote split) and less partisan than were regulatory or redistributive issues.

More specific measures for the substantive areas were incorporated. The six issue-areas proved more salient on the indicators of assertiveness, conflict, and support than for the benchmark all votes in Congress. Presidents were more assertive, as expected, on public works and the two redistributive areas (civil rights and poverty) than on the regulatory areas. Price supports was the most controversial and partisan issue-area. Crime scored lowest on these two related indicators. Although somewhat less than for all votes, Presidents still received high legislative support. Support was greatest for civil rights (86 percent), but still high at 60 percent for public works, the issue-area receiving the lowest level of legislative support.

The environmental variables generally revealed differences across policy areas. Democrats were more assertive on all areas but antitrust. This issue-area was also the only one where there were more party line votes under Republican than Democratic Presidents. While votes were more conflictual under Democratic Presidents, they still received greater support than Republicans for their positions, especially in public works and antitrust. As with all other votes, Presidents were more assertive on the issue-areas during their last year in office and least so in their first year (as compared to reelection year for all votes). Last year also exhibited more controversial votes, except for antitrust and civil rights, which were more controversial during Presidents' first year in office. Election years elicited the greatest partisan vote split for public works, crime, and poverty and the least for the other three policy areas (price supports, antitrust, and civil rights). Presidents obtain their greatest support during reelections and least support during first years, especially for price supports, antitrust, and civil rights. Only in public works do Presidents obtain considerably higher support during their first years in office.

Although the data for each of the six Presidents across substantive areas have not been provided, some of the permutations and implications for all six policy areas combined can be summarized. With the exception of Johnson, little difference appeared in position-taking among the other five Presidents. Yet Johnson did no better in obtaining Congressional support for his positions than did Carter, and, he fared worse than Kennedy. The latter clearly wanted Congressional wins to bolster a faltering legislative reputation. Support was fairly stable over time, largely a function of Presidents' party. Conflict declined over time; indeed, partisanship was greatest for Eisenhower and least for Nixon. Despite a general decline in party voting in Congress, we assume some posturing. Eisenhower took positions on a high proportion of votes, while Nixon obviously shied away from those that were most controversial. What was observed was considerable variation among Presidents, but the reasons for variation are not always suggested by these aggregate measures. Many qualitative factors like style and skill are missed but, of course, may not be easily accounted for (Edwards 1980, Ch. 7).

The findings in this chapter give little confidence that Congress has the will to lead the President in domestic policy formation. Modification can occur through informal contacts, committee, and floor actions. Our measures of floor action revealed little modification by Congress. The resources for Presidential leadership were limited during the 1970s by a reassertive Congress, but the balance of power has not dramatically shifted. None of the primarily negative reforms of the era, not even the Budget Control and Impoundment Act, has succeeded in providing the unified, comprehensive perspective that would enable Congress to compete more equally with the President.

The following chapter completes the policy formation cycle. Is Congress as unassertive in adopting Presidents' policies as it was revealed to be in their modification? We expect more Congressional scrutiny in adoption because all the issues are Presidentially inspired ones, not the legislatively derived roll calls that constitute our data base in policy modification. Therefore Congress's leadership potential seems greater in policy adoption.

NOTES

1. Interested readers should consult some of the standard texts for greater detail on Presidential and Congressional resources. See, for example, Cronin 1980; Edwards 1980; Shull 1979a; Wayne 1978.

2. Authors disagree over the relative percentage of bills originating in the Executive branch. Although Schwarz and Shaw contend that it was less

than 50 percent from 1963 through 1972 (1976, 230), figures of 80 percent and even 95 percent have been offered. Others discussing the tendency for policy to originate from the Executive include Robinson 1967 and Huntington 1961.

3. Obviously no single measure fully gets at Presidential support (or Congressional modification). A more detailed discussion of the properties of this and related indicators is provided in Chapter 5 and the Methodological Appendix.

4. Because only two years are available for last years, caution must be exercised in its interpretation.

5. Spitzer (1980) incorporates differing indicators of partisanship and conflict for functional areas. The only party differences he offers are by Presidential Administration. In addition to this measure, I provide for substantive areas an indicator of partisanship in Congress: number of roll calls evoking party splits in voting. The conflict measures also differ. Spitzer's measure for functional areas is the unanimity on each vote. A noncontroversial vote is one with 90 percent or greater agreement (1980, 26). The conflict measure used here for substantive areas is mean vote split (see Appendix). Generally more specific indicators are provided for substantive policy areas.

6. The latter project goes back even further than this. The idea of such a waterway was criticized by an engineer in 1874 (*National Journal*, April 7, 1979, 570).

7. Unlike Presidential position-taking (assertiveness) overall, Congressional Quarterly does not provide sufficient information to identify such votes for specific issue-areas prior to 1957.

8. In the interest of conserving space, I will not discuss these variables in detail by individual Presidents. Only the findings are summarized; the data may be obtained from the author.

Adoption   5

CONGRESSIONAL LEADERSHIP
FROM LEGITIMATION

Policy adoption is the culmination of the policy formation process. Whether or not it modifies Presidential preferences, Congress makes the ultimate determination of Presidential policies. Thus, it plays a legitimizing role in its decisions to adopt Presidential requests. Congress can initiate policy itself and adopt its own initiatives, but we are concerned here with the level of its acceptance of Presidential requests, labeled success. In adopting Presidential policies, Congress is legitimizing them, whereas with modification, Congress may merely change or accede to Presidential actions. Both support (modification) and success (adoption) are Congressional prerogatives; they both also are indicators of the relative power of the President vis-à-vis Congress.[1] By measuring power relationships, the two variables also help us understand leadership.

The primary manifestation of Presidential leadership over Congress is the extent to which Congress accedes to his wishes. Perhaps the biggest hurdle Presidents face is gaining acceptance of their policy initiatives. Looking at Presidential success from 1948 through 1964, Wildavsky (1966) found that Congress approved approximately 50 percent of Presidents' proposals but at a significantly higher percentage in defense and foreign policy than in the domestic area. An update of this information through 1975 suggests little change. About half of Presidents' initiatives still are approved by Congress, although the gap between foreign and domestic initiatives seems to be narrowing (LeLoup and Shull 1979a). If Congress continues to give the President less than half of what he asks for in the domestic realm, who really leads?

Congressional or Presidential Leadership?

The essence of the President's political leadership over Congress is his ability to persuade. "All Presidents wish they could make Congress serve them as a rubber-stamp, converting their agendas into prompt enactments, and most Presidents will try to bring that miracle about, whenever and as best they can" (Neustadt 1973, 136). Thomas Jefferson was the first President to provide sustained leadership over Congress, a leadership that was very strong and even involved selection of his party's Congressional leaders. The first unelected President, John Tyler, was the all-time champion of bad relations with Congress, and even with his own cabinet (Gallagher 1974, 221). Many of his problems appear attributable to his arrogance and abrasive personality.

The emergence of the modern Presidency did not greatly change relations with Congress. If anything, Presidents became even more assertive. Theodore Roosevelt, Woodrow Wilson, and Franklin Roosevelt are often credited with being aggressive leaders in their relations with Congress. Theodore Roosevelt, for example, stated, "I refused to recognize the right of Congress to interfere with me excepting by impeachment or in another constitutional matter" (Andrews 1958, 200).

More recent Presidents have also asserted leadership but in a less antagonistic fashion. Nevertheless, they made it clear that they believed such leadership was well within their rights. A Carter campaign statement, which he later regretted, said:

The nation is best served by a strong, independent, and aggressive President, working with a strong and independent Congress. . . . I have the greatest respect for Congress, but I don't consider the Congress to be inherently capable of leadership. I think the Founding Fathers expected the President to be the leader of the Country. [Quoted in *National Journal*, 1/15/77, 91]

Congressional adoption (legitimation) of Presidential initiatives helps us clarify relations between the executive and legislative branches and the extent to which the President leads Congress, or vice-versa. This indicator of success reveals areas of Presidential strength and Congressional independence. There is no question that the success measure provides an incomplete picture of Presidential relations with Congress; however, most domestic issues do require approval by Congress, and the variable should shed light on these actor interactions and power relations.

How is Legitimation Determined?

While keeping the methodological discussion to a minimum and relegating much of it to the Appendix, we now briefly introduce the measure of success. Legitimation refers to Congressional adoption of the President's legislative requests (initiatives from Chapter 3). This box score measure, available from Congressional Quarterly from 1953 through 1975, is essentially the President's success rate. Considerable debate has arisen over the advantages of various measures of Presidential-Congressional relations. Certainly there are difficulties with all such measures, as scholars have documented (Edwards 1980, 50-53; LeLoup and Shull 1979a, 708; Peppers 1975; Ripley 1972; 1979, 69; Shull 1979a, 1981; Sigelman 1979; and Wayne 1978, 168-71).

No single quantitative measure of Presidential-Congressional relations is perfect. Qualitative indicators could be just as important, but they are difficult to obtain. The meaning of these measures is not always clear; success and support, for example, are often confused (see Appendix). Also, environmental circumstances intervene, such as the following: Where do the President's interests lie? What are Congressional expectations? What is the philosophical and/or partisan composition of Congress and the White House? How popular is the President, and at what stage is he in his term of office? These questions are addressed after first examining overall success. Because aggregate measures may not totally measure reality and may even be inconclusive (Ripley 1979, 69), we then compare success in conjunction with support (from Chapter 4) and also consider some of the possible environmental influences on legislative modification and adoption.

ADOPTION OVERALL

The data on legislative adoption (success) are compared later in the chapter with support, but the yearly overall figures may be previewed in Figure 5-1. A cursory look at the data reveals that these approval rates vary somewhat but are relatively stable over the period of the study. There are two exceptions to this stability:

the first two (relatively inactive) years of the Eisenhower Administration, when Eisenhower enjoyed his only Republican majority in Congress, and the 1965-66 period when the Eighty-ninth Congress approved a historically large proportion of Johnson's requests. Thus, the highest approval rates were for Eisenhower in 1953 when he had the fewest proposals and for Johnson in 1965 when he had the most. With this exception of Johnson, however, little relationship is evident between approval rate and number of initiatives proposed ($r = .24$).

Besides activism (as measured by number of initiatives), success probably is also a function of party, year, and characteristics of individual Presidents. Related research has established that Democrats, due largely to their Congressional party majorities, obtained greater success overall (51 percent) than did Republicans (40 percent) (LeLoup and Shull 1979b, 15). Approval rates broken down by individual Presidents also reveal considerable variation, with a range of 57 percent of initiatives approved under Johnson to just 31 percent under Ford.

No measure of success is available after 1975; thus quantitative comparisons for Carter and Reagan are not possible. However, we are able to construct qualitative and tentative judgments through interviews and news accounts. Carter was moderately successful with his legislative package in his first two years. Approved were an Energy Department, increased minimum wage, government reorganization authority, farm price supports, social security revisions, an economic stimulus package, an energy package, and a full employment act. The President failed to get election reform, a consumer protection agency, health costs containment, and half of the water projects he had recommended be eliminated. Carter obtained approval of most of his foreign policy proposals but continued to be rebuffed on many domestic and economic issues. Of Carter's six domestic priorities in 1979 (confidential interview), only one, the Department of Education, passed Congress. One author documents twenty-one initiatives approved by Congress (Ripley 1979, 70). Other assessments of the Carter record are more positive. Legislative aide Dan Tate claimed the President had obtained a 75 to 85 percent approval record (*National Journal*, 11/3/79, 1856), and George Edwards, using other measures, asserts that Carter's support (at least from senators in 1977-78) was better than all other postwar Presidents and at least equal to Johnson's

(1980, 193). Harvey Zeidenstein finds Carter obtaining the greatest support on key votes (if not success on initiatives) of any other President in foreign policy (1981, 511).

Judgments about Reagan are more tenuous. Most attention in 1981 centered on his success in obtaining tax and budget cuts. Despite Reagan's enormous first year success in these areas, important questions about his leadership emerged (Broder 1982, 11), and Congress provided greater scrutiny thereafter. Reagan did not obtain approval during 1982 on constitutional amendments banning abortion or requiring balanced budgets. He also failed during a special session late in that year to achieve some of his priorities such as the MX missile.

Success and Support

The Congressional Quarterly organization provides measures of Presidential success and support with Congress. But in failing to recognize the quite different nature of the two measures, authors have frequently used them interchangeably. Support is derived from legislative roll calls on which the President takes a position; thus, they are Congressionally sponsored. The roll call support measure, then, is a Congressional response not to Presidential policy but merely to his position on a particular issue before Congress. The Presidents' motivation for supporting particular legislative issues is unknown and changeable. It may be, as with Kennedy, that the President wants to go along—that he takes few positions, and when he does, they tend to be on issues popular in Congress. These votes on which positions are based may or may not be on Presidential initiatives and are irrespective of whether the issue passes. Success, on the other hand, is based on initiatives to Congress that come from Presidents themselves.

Figure 5-1 shows that these two measures seem similar but evidence different patterns ($r = .61$). What is observed, however, is that support levels average considerably higher than success. The fact that Lee Sigelman (1979) finds less support for major issues (even quite a bit lower than the success measure) shows that key votes are highly controversial (and therefore atypical) compared to most initiatives, or particularly, to most nonkey roll calls. Existing research already focuses too much on unique phenomena, as typified by Sigelman's key votes. The indicators of success and support

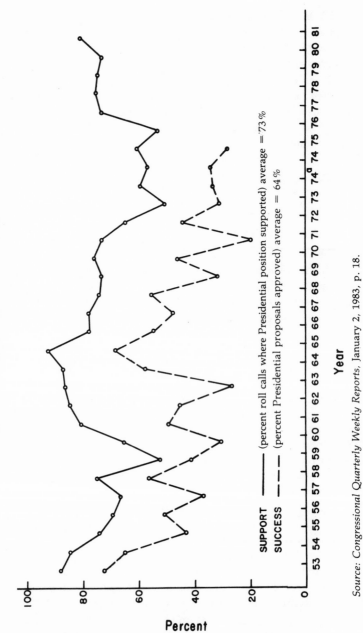

Figure 5-1. Congressional Success and Support

SUPPORT ———— (percent roll calls where Presidential position supported) average = '73%

SUCCESS — — — (percent Presidential proposals approved) average = 64%

Percent

Year

Source: Congressional Quarterly Weekly Reports, January 2, 1983, p. 18.

[a]Nixon.

comprise a broader spectrum of policy preferences, encompassing both routine and controversial matters.

Presidents averaged only 44 percent of their proposals approved (success), but their overall support from Congress on votes where they took an identifiable position was much higher (73 percent). All Presidents fared better on support than success. Why should this be? A proposal by the President must pass both houses to be approved. His position on a roll call, however, often refers to a vote in either chamber.[2] In addition, roll calls normally occur on final passage of legislation, while many proposals never get out of committee.

Conditions for Support and Success

Numerous circumstances affect Congressional approval of Presidential positions (support) and of his proposals (success). These include elections and public opinion, timing, partisanship in Congress, and the nature of Congressional party leadership.

Elections and Public Opinion

Presidential elections can be expected to make a difference in success and support. According to Edwards, elections "provide a vehicle through which the public can express its general views to a Congressman and can have an effect on Congressional behavior without having detailed views on specific policies" (1978, 167). The influence of Presidential elections is particularly important if it has been a significant victory. Thus, it can be hypothesized that the greater the President's election percentage, the greater his success and support (Cohen 1980). This explanation is confounded, however, because Nixon's equally impressive margin in 1972 relative to Johnson's in 1964 brought them widely differing success levels. Cohen also speculates that nonelected Presidents fare less well than those elected to office (1980, 19).

Legislative support is also related to public support for the President. It has been suggested (at least for northern Democrats and southern Republicans) that the greater the President's popularity in a Congressman's district, the greater the likelihood of success and support (Edwards 1978). Surely, high popularity overall and positive media attention should also contribute to better Congressional relations (Shinn 1980; Edwards 1980). Obviously a decline in

Presidential prestige (such as Nixon by spring of 1973) affects Presidents' success and support. Other examples of Presidential popularity and changes in legislative relations can be observed.

Timing

The timing of issues can have extremely important consequences for their prospects of Congressional passage. Some Presidents will dodge action, but most will advocate programs and take positions on legislation that will maximize their support during crises and other conditions (such as occasional public outrages or euphoria). Their success rate is quite volatile from year to year (Hammond and Fraser 1980, 41). Approval is more likely at the beginning of an Administration rather than later, especially if the President is a lame duck (Light 1982). Thus, the earlier in the President's term, the greater his success and support. Table 5-1 finds support for the hypothesis for Eisenhower and Kennedy on success, but the differences are small for Johnson and Nixon. The missing data for the other Presidents do not allow confirmation. An average of 49 percent of Presidents' first year proposals are approved by Congress compared to only 37 percent for those during their last year in office, however, lending some credence to the proposition. The data are more convincing for support; most Presidents received greater support in their first year of office than in their last year.[3] Reagan got off to an unusually good start in 1981 (see Table 5-1).

Party Margins

The extent of Presidential support in Congress is also conditioned by party in the White House, as well as legislative party margins. Presidents attempt both to exert influence over members of their party and to seek their support. Political party affiliation acts as a unifier of partisans in Congress, since the party occupying the White House normally has more cohesive voting. We can hypothesize that the greater the proportion of the President's partisans in Congress, the greater his legislative success (Hammond and Fraser 1980; Shinn 1980; Zeidenstein 1981, 511). The proportion of Democrats in Congress from 1933 through 1983 is provided in Figure 5-2. When the President's party is in control of Congress, he gets his way about 85 percent of the time but only

Table 5-1. Comparison of Congressional Support and Success

President	Percent Support	Percent Success	First Year	Percent Support	Percent Success	Last Year
Eisenhower	89	73	1953	65	31	1960
Kennedy	81	48	1961	87	27	1963
Johnson	88	58	1964	75	56	1968
Nixon	74	32	1969	60	34	1974
Ford	58	36	1974	53	—	1976
Carter	75	—	1977	75	—	1980
Reagan	82	—	1981	—	—	—
Overall Average	78	49		69	37	

Source: <u>Congressional Quarterly Weekly Reports</u> (January 2, 1982, 18).

Figure 5-2. Size of Democratic Majority in Congress

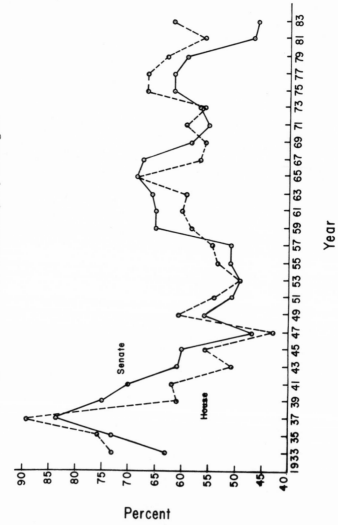

Year

Percent

Source: *Congressional Quarterly Weekly Reports* (yearly).

about 65 percent when his party has minority status in Congress (Jacob 1977, 101). Since Democrats have controlled Congress with few exceptions since 1933, it is not surprising that both support and success for Democratic Presidents are higher than for Republicans.

Party Leadership

A mutual dependence exists between the President and his party leaders in Congress. "Failure to involve Congressional leaders adequately at a sufficiently early stage can spell the defeat of the President's legislative program" (Thomas 1975, 181). His Congressional party leaders need him too because in order to have influence with their colleagues, they must appear to be the President's Congressional spokesmen. They must walk a fine line between their support (but not oversupport) of the President's interests and their attachment and loyalty to Congress (Truman 1959, 179-80; 1969, 463). In general, it is expected that party leaders tend to have higher Presidential support and opposition scores than do rank-and-file party members (Shull 1979a, 100; Shinn 1980).

Assessment

The above and other environmental conditions have explained upward of 90 percent of the variance in Congressional support of the President. Interest groups and White House liaison should also affect support and success. Presidents, however, are greatly limited in their ability to control such external conditions as the economy or such internal legislative conditions as factionalism and member stability or vote. John Kingdon asserts that the President has minimal influence on 61 percent of Congressional voting (1981, 177-78). While we saw limited modification of Presidential positions in Chapter 4, substantially lower adoption of his legislative requests is evident here (see Figure 5-1). Despite limited opportunity to influence his support and success with Congress, a President's personal activity, timing, and working with party leaders does seem to help his Congressional relations. A determined President can make a difference, if not necessarily lead Congress in domestic policymaking.

Beyond these differences in support and success overall, and by environmental conditions, it is believed that there are even greater differences by policy area. Is it possible to distinguish between a distributive and a regulatory Presidency, or a civil rights and a public works Presidency? Are variations across domestic areas greater or less than differences observed between domestic and foreign policy (Wildavsky 1966; LeLoup and Shull 1979a)? Although several domestic areas were identified by the latter authors, what about the frequently narrower ones incorporated here? And if such dimensions can be observed, are they fairly stable over time? We hope to find an extension of an observation in an earlier work: "concealed beneath the rubric of domestic policy may be significant variations in how Congress responds to presidential proposals" (LeLoup and Shull 1979a, 707). We now turn to this examination, first for functional areas, and then for the six substantive areas of domestic policy.

FUNCTIONAL AREAS

In discussing the findings for both functional and substantive policy areas, we shall follow the pattern established in previous chapters: summary of the policy content, overview of findings on success overall and by policy area, and then by the environmental variables (Presidents individually, by political party, and then by selected years in Presidential terms of office).

Content of Adopted Policies

Distributive issues constituted the largest and most diverse group of initiatives and legislative responses. Proposals like health and housing grants and construction did best in terms of Congressional passage. Johnson did quite well on many other issues, such as agriculture, veterans, and urban development. Distributive issues that fared the poorest were mostly in the resources area: public works, agriculture, parks, and energy development.[4] Transportation, communications, and construction suffered declining success with Congress. Most Presidents had difficulty obtaining Congressional approval for distributive programs in education or for the aged.[5]

Regulatory issues with fairly high Presidential success included the economy, trade, and labor issues. Particularly successful were economic issues under Eisenhower and Ford, election reform under

Kennedy and Johnson, crime under Johnson and Ford, and environmental and energy regulation under Nixon and Ford. Since the energy issue became important in the early 1970s, Presidents, obviously including Carter, have not received a high level of approval from Congress. By early 1983, Congress had not approved Reagan's efforts to dismantle the Department of Energy and deregulate natural gas.

Redistributive subissues seemed to vary more in terms of legislative approval. Although Eisenhower obtained support for most of his civil rights initiatives, Johnson and Nixon did not. Of course, more civil rights proposals were initiated by them than by Eisenhower. Welfare issues frequently were a nemesis for Presidents (except Johnson and Kennedy), as was taxation (except for Nixon). Although Kennedy did well on both welfare and foreign aid, Nixon did not. The issue of immigration was particularly controversial in the 1950s and early 1960s—an issue on which Congress exercised control and seldom gave Presidents their preferred policies.

Overview of Functional Areas

Figure 5-3 shows how successful Presidents were in obtaining their initiatives overall and in each functional area. Less than one-half (45 percent) of the 4,438 categorized initiatives from 1953 through 1975 were approved by Congress. As expected, Presidents received substantially higher support for distributive policies (51 percent) than for those that were regulatory (37 percent) or redistributive (44 percent). The values in Figure 5-3 give considerable confidence in this conclusion, although the statistical association is modest.[6] The expectation of greater approval over time for regulatory requests was not confirmed. Indeed, Congress increasingly has perceived regulatory issues as subject to its scrutiny.

Environmental Conditions

Presidents Individually

Considerable differences in success are evident among the five Presidents for which data are available. Eisenhower had the greatest success of any other President on regulatory policy (see

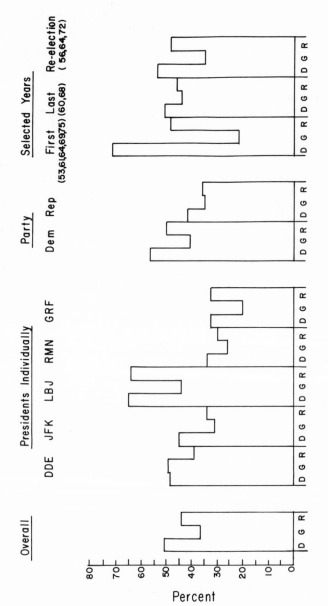

Figure 5-3. Congressional Success (by Functional Areas)

Note: D = distributive; G = regulatory; R = redistributive.

Figure 5-3). Overall he received a higher portion of his initiatives (47 percent) than any other President but Johnson. Unlike his support scores, Kennedy fared poorly on legislative success, barely outdistancing Nixon and Ford. He received particularly low success on his redistributive policies. Johnson was the single President of this group able to obtain approval on more than half of all his initiatives (58 percent). Compared to the mean success rates, Johnson was particularly successful in redistributive policy. Nixon's and Ford's success was much lower than average overall and in each policy area. Nixon achieved higher success than Ford on regulatory initiatives but did poorly on redistributive ones. Ford's overall success (31 percent), with a dismal 20 percent approval on regulatory policy, was lowest among contemporary Presidents (see Figure 5-3).

Party

Democrats did substantially better overall and in every policy area than Republican Presidents. Obviously this greater success is attributable to Johnson rather than Kennedy. Yet Nixon, and particularly Ford, did little to help the success of Republican Presidents. We had expected greatest party differences in redistributive and regulatory policies and least on distributive because the latter normally calls for less change. Although redistributive policy was controversial as anticipated, it was the distributive policy area that generated the greatest partisan differences in success (see Figure 5-3). Partisanship, then, seems more pervasive in this policy area, at least for Congressional success, than many other authors have claimed (Lowi 1964; Ripley and Franklin 1980).

Year

Selected years also discriminated among the three functional policy areas, at least for distributive and regulatory issues. Essentially no yearly differences could be discerned in adoption rates for redistributive policy (see Figure 5-3). Distributive policies were approved much more frequently during first year than last year; the opposite was true for regulatory policy. Presidents experienced very little first year scrutiny on the former, but that was when Congress was exceptionally strict in disallowing regulatory initiatives. Even Lyndon Johnson obtained only six of his twenty-two proposed regulatory initiatives in 1964.

SUBSTANTIVE AREAS

We now examine how the substantive policy areas fare on Congressional success. What types of Presidential requests are adopted by Congress? Has the substance of these issue-areas varied over time, and how do they compare to functional areas? Are they similar in success to those that are conceptually similar? How well do the environmental conditions discriminate among the policy areas on Congressional success? In order to tap this last question more fully, we include consideration of the two subissue areas provided in Chapter 3: water projects and school desegregation.

Content of Adopted Policies

Price Supports

Although Eisenhower experienced inordinately high success on price supports requests, a Presidential-Congressional stalemate on specific agricultural issues developed during the later years of his Administration (Anderson, Brady, and Bullock, 1978, 379). With the exception of corn in 1958, Eisenhower was generally frustrated in his attempts to reduce acreage allotments or to increase the discretion of the Secretary of Agriculture in setting price support levels. Kennedy was even less successful in obtaining his agricultural initiatives. He too was rebuffed in requests to expand the power of the Secretary of Agriculture and in his positions on acreage allotments, except when he pushed for higher levels.

Johnson also was often disappointed in his agricultural requests, especially when he tried to make the programs more redistributive (for example, creation of a national food bank and more aid to small producers). Johnson was successful in 1965 in increasing the wheat parity to 100 percent and in extension of the Wool Act. But like his predecessors, Johnson was unable to obtain greater discretion for the Department of Agriculture. Johnson obtained approval on none of his 1968 initiatives. Nixon's low level of success is exemplified by failing efforts to remove production controls and acreage allotments, particularly in 1974, for such southern crops as cotton, peanuts, and rice.

Public Works

Because of the huge number of public works initiatives, we center our discussion of policy content on water projects only.

Most of Eisenhower's requests dealt with specific projects, where he was usually unsuccessful. For example, his attempts to secure the Fryingpan-Arkansas project failed during four different years. Throughout the second half of his Administration, Eisenhower tried unsuccessfully to reduce many programs and even to limit Army Corps of Engineers projects to those already begun.

Kennedy continually, without success, tried to establish a water resources council and grants in aid to help in planning water resources. In 1964, Johnson sought and achieved Kennedy's earlier proposal of a land and water conservation fund (Public Law No. 578). During 1965, Johnson was successful on nearly all of his requests but was denied his request for a power plant at the Grand Coulee Dam and a national wilderness rivers system. Although he received increased aid to the states, Johnson was unable to gain either greater executive control of water policy or fees for users of the nation's waterways. The latter issue reemerged as a Reagan initiative in 1981-82.

Nixon and Ford were less assertive on water projects. Nixon did not obtain increases in funding for scenic rivers (1972) or development of the resources of estuaries (1970). A cynic might allude to the unusually large number of initiatives during 1970-73 directed toward the coastal states of Florida and California, where the President owned property. Ford obtained support for a Maritime Administration authorization. Reassertions by Carter and Reagan on water projects were not noticeably successful. During 1982, Reagan pushed, to no avail, to have the states share up to 35 percent of the costs of water projects.

Crime

Most of Eisenhower's successful crime initiatives dealt with internal security. Kennedy was frustrated in his initiatives for drug laws and a continuation of the 1961 Juvenile Delinquency Act. The act was extended in 1964 under Johnson (Public Law No. 368). Major requests approved under Johnson include the Law Enforcement Assistance Administration (1965), Bail Reform Act (1966), Narcotics Enforcement Training Program (1967), and in 1968 the Federal Anti-Riot Act, Juvenile Delinquency Prevention Act, and the Safe Streets Crime and Control Act. Yet many of Johnson's crime initiatives were not adopted: aid for state and local governments, outlawing wiretapping, and banning over-the-counter sales of handguns. Johnson was able to prohibit the interstate mail order shipment of firearms (Public Law No. 618).

Nixon was the first President to push hard against organized crime. Although rebuffed in 1969, he obtained the Organized Crime Control Act of 1970 (Public Law No. 452). Nixon also gained approval from Congress for many of his efforts aimed at drug abuse. In his remaining years in office, he was defeated on such initiatives as restoring the death penalty, reforming the criminal code, and legislation against disruptions of political campaigns. Nixon received approval on none of his eight initiatives in 1973, and Ford was never successful on a single one of his 1975 crime initiatives. Reagan's numerous initiatives in September 1982 (for example, to limit appeals from state to federal courts and to allow greater use of evidence obtained) seemed unlikely to pass.

Antitrust

Eisenhower's success on antitrust was mixed. He obtained increases in fines for antitrust violators (1955), regulation of holding companies (1956), and application of antitrust regulations to bank mergers (1960, Public Law No. 463). But he failed to achieve many other initiatives, such as increasing FTC jurisdiction, requiring advance notice of mergers, and making cease and desist orders final. Kennedy's few initiatives, dealing with the powers of the FTC, were unsuccessful. Johnson also had few antitrust initiatives. Although he obtained approval for greater enforcement power, he also sought and was granted exemptions from antitrust laws to support U.S. balance of payments in 1965. Nixon successfully ended the practice of allowing multiple subsidiaries and affiliated corporations to receive undue tax breaks (1969). His plans to increase the effectiveness of the FTC were not realized, however. Ford secured an amendment to the Interstate Commerce Act to allow anticompetitive railroad rate practices.[7]

Civil Rights

As was the case in Chapter 3, we concentrate on the subissue of school desegregation. Eisenhower's modest initiatives were unsuccessful until the final year of his Administration, when obstructing court-ordered desegregation was made a crime (Public Law No. 449). Kennedy also requested no legislation until his final year in office. He asked Congress to allow the Attorney General to initiate suits for noncompliance, but no such legislation passed, despite the urgings of Kennedy and his successor, Lyndon Johnson. Although Johnson was not able to achieve a request for financial aid to local governments, he did obtain Public Law No. 284 (1968), prohibiting interference with minorities who were attending a private school or college. Nixon failed to get an equal educational opportunity act in 1972 and continued, unsuccessfully, the initiative of his predecessors to grant aid to local schools attempting to desegregate. Such legislation finally passed in 1974 but contained an amendment prohibiting court-ordered busing under certain circumstances. Civil rights received more attention, but not necessarily more success, under the divergent policies of Carter and Reagan (LeLoup and Shull 1982).

Poverty

Because of the large number of poverty initiatives, we focus the discussion of policy on housing. Eisenhower usually gained approval for his housing initiatives. The number of public housing units steadily increased, although Congressional support declined by 1958, when a request simply extending the same number of housing units as had existed for four years (70,000) was defeated. In 1959 Eisenhower did win special mortgage insurance for displaced families (Public Law No. 372). Although housing subsequently took a back seat to other poverty programs, Kennedy established federally insured loans for rural housing. Johnson obtained assistance for the housing problems of farm laborers (1964, 1967), rent supplement programs for low-income families (1965-66), and the Housing and Urban Development Act of 1968 (Public Law No. 448). Johnson was not always the winner, however. He was denied permission to purchase public housing stock or to allow local authorization to lease additional housing units.

Nixon and Ford were thwarted in their desire to consolidate welfare programs, specifically in housing. Nixon sought unsuccessfully to move toward a cash assistance approach in 1973. None of Ford's initiatives on housing were approved. Like Nixon, Reagan favored a rent voucher system instead of federally subsidized housing units. He sought huge reductions (at least $600 million in fiscal 1982) in housing subsidy funds. Reagan's proposed voucher plan was rejected by Congress in 1981 but was reintroduced in modified form late in 1982 in preparation for the fiscal 1984 budget request. Neither Carter nor Reagan obtained approval of comprehensive welfare initiatives.

Overview of Substantive Areas

Just half of the seventeen hundred or so initiatives in these six policy areas were adopted by Congress. Despite their salience, this figure actually is slightly better than success for all domestic initiatives during this period. As might be expected, there is considerable variation across issue-areas in approval rates, ranging from a high of 62 percent for poverty to a low of 24 percent for antitrust initiatives (see Figure 5-4). The findings were somewhat analogous to the discussion of functional areas (least success on regulatory issues). Despite the rather low adoption rate for civil rights (33 percent), poverty gives the two representatives of redistributive policy much higher success than we observed overall. The two distributive areas (price supports and public works) both obtained about average success. Therefore the fit between substantive and functional areas is imperfect. We now consider the results of success on substantive areas, controlling for the environmental influences.

Environmental Conditions

Presidents Individually

Success on these issue-areas combined approximated that for all domestic initiatives—that is, greatest success for Johnson (57 percent) and least for Ford (30 percent). This success is largely attributable to huge Congressional majorities for the former and minorities for the latter. Eisenhower obtained a slightly higher proportion of initiatives than Kennedy (43 to 41 percent). However, price supports accounted for nearly all of his successes; indeed, his rate there and on crime was the highest of any other President. Eisenhower's success on other issue-areas (such as antitrust, civil rights, and poverty) was quite low (see Figure 5-4).

Kennedy achieved zero success on his few antitrust and crime initiatives and obtained by far the least success of any other Presi-

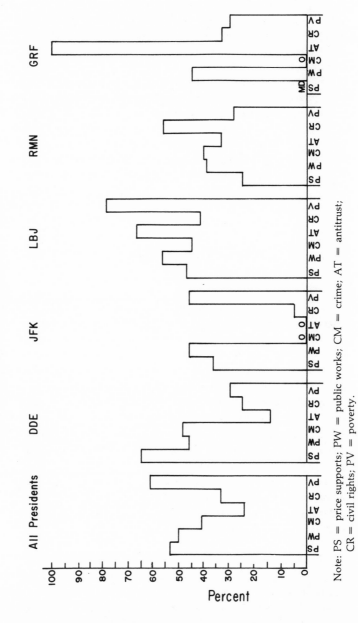

Figure 5-4. Congressional Success (by Presidents)

Note: PS = price supports; PW = public works; CM = crime; AT = antitrust;
CR = civil rights; PV = poverty.

dent on civil rights, perhaps because his few civil rights initiatives were quite liberal. At the same time, he was fairly successful with his poverty initiatives, although Johnson was the grand champion there, with approval of 78 percent of his initiatives (see Figure 5-4). Johnson's success carried over into other policy areas too, such as public works and antitrust.

The contrast between Johnson and his two successors is substantial. Nixon's 37 percent overall approval on these areas conceals considerable differences among policy areas. He obtained the least success of any other President on his conservative poverty positions; however, if Congress was fairly liberal on poverty, it was growing more conservative on civil rights when it approved a higher proportion (56 percent) of Nixon initiatives than for any other President (see Figure 5-4). Ford made so few requests that cautious interpretation is necessary, notably for antitrust, where his 100 percent success is based upon a single initiative. On four of the other policy areas, we have substantially more requests. He had no success at all on crime (see Figure 5-4).

Party

Fairly substantial party differences appear when we look at success on these six areas overall: 53 percent success for Democrats versus 40 percent for Republicans. Party differences are considerable on price supports, antitrust, and poverty; virtually no differences in success are evident for civil rights (see Figure 5-5), probably because the Democratic party was deeply divided on the issue-area, particularly during the 1960s. Price supports was the only area where Republican Presidents did better than Democrats (largely attributable to Eisenhower). The control for party gives us pause about the fit of the six substantive areas to the Lowi typology, since each pair within the three functional categories performed differently on success as a function of the party affiliation of the President. Only three of the policy areas showed considerable partisan differences in success, and each was within a different Lowi category.

Year

There are virtually no differences in success on these six issue-areas combined during reelection years (54 percent), last years in office (52 percent), and first years (50 percent). Differences are more pronounced when the policy areas are examined separately.

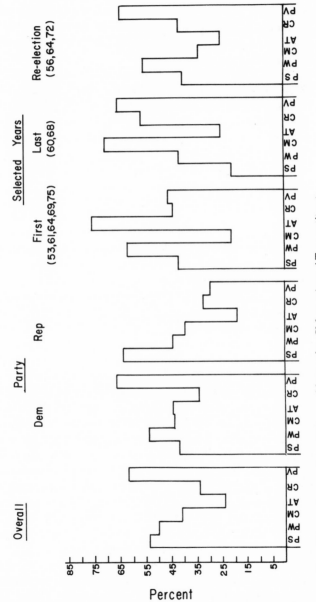

Figure 5-5. Congressional Success (by Environmental Variables)

Note: PS = price supports; PW = public works; CM = crime; AT = antitrust;
CR = civil rights; PV = poverty.

Presidents actually did better during their first years in price supports, public works, and especially antitrust (see Figure 5-5). First year success was much lower for crime and poverty. Contrary to their first year support, distributive issues did poorly during last years. On the other hand, crime and the two redistributive issue-areas (civil rights and poverty) obtained their highest success during Presidents' last years. It is ironic that success overall was highest during reelection years despite the fact that individual success on none of the six areas was highest then. The explanation is that reelection year support was nearly as high as first year support for price supports and public works and almost as high as last year support for poverty. Success on civil rights was lowest for reelection years among selected years (see Figure 5-5).

Two Subareas

As was done in Chapter 3 for Presidential initiatives, it is possible to provide a more detailed look at subissues within the broader policy areas by examining legislative success on the two previously identified subareas: water projects within public works and school desegregation within civil rights.

Water Projects

A smaller proportion of water projects was approved (45 percent) than was the case for its broader public works category. Kennedy obtained the least success (24 percent), while Ford's was highest, (based upon only three initiatives) (see Figure 5-6). Johnson achieved most of his requests for water projects, and Nixon, Johnson, and Ford all did better on this seemingly controversial subarea than for public works as a whole. Such success on water projects did not hold true for the more controversial requests made by Carter and Reagan.

Party and selected year differences in success were less for water projects than they had been for the larger public works area. Democrats fared only slightly better (47 percent) than Republicans (43 percent). Presidents were most successful in reelection years, although for public works as a whole, they obtained their greatest success during their first year in office. The lowest proportion of initiatives on water projects to be approved occurred during last years in Presidential terms (see Figure 5-6).

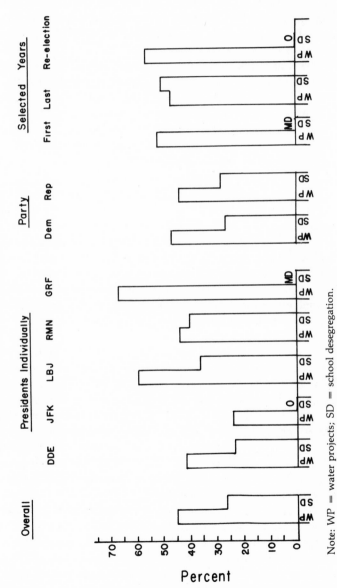

Figure 5-6. Congressional Success (by Subissue Areas)

Note: WP = water projects; SD = school desegregation.

School Desegregation

School desegregation was also more controversial than its broader civil rights area since only 27 percent of Presidential requests were approved by Congress. Nixon and Johnson were most successful, while Kennedy received none of his four school desegregation requests (see Figure 5-6).

The controversy on school desegregation was not due to partisan control of the White House, as no such differences in success emerged. Unfortunately, the data points are so few for selected years that we can make only tentative judgments. About the only observation possible is that Presidents are fairly successful during their last years in office (see Figure 5-6), just as they had been for the larger civil rights policy area as a whole.

Policy adoption along with policy modification helps us understand leadership. Because most policy in the domestic realm requires Congressional action, Congress has the last word and may be capable of exerting a leadership role as it legitimizes Presidential policies.[8] Because the two actors must interact, Congress and the President share power in the final stage of domestic policy formation. Congress can initiate on its own and "takes the lead often enough on a range of policy matters that are serious enough to give it a place of distinction as a genuine policy-maker and innovator" (Johannes 1972a, 5).

If Congressional assertiveness can occur earlier in the process, it is particularly evident at the end of policy formation with the adoption of Presidents' legislative requests, the measure of success. Despite some limitations with the measure documented in this chapter and in the Methodological Appendix, success examines an important, if different, dimension of Presidential-Congressional relations than do other measures used here and elsewhere. Success, for example, was shown to be both similar to and different from support, but the conceptual differences in these indicators are probably greater than can be measured.

Legislative approval rates vary enormously over time and seem to be conditioned by a number of factors. Success is not simply a function of number of initiatives (Presidential assertiveness). It is probable that some of the environmental circumstances (the economy and interest group support), as well as conditions more under Presidential control (personal intervention and liaison), affect Presidential success specifically and Congressional relations generally. Congress reveals increasing scrutiny in adopting Presidential policies, especially when recent conservatives (Republicans) have occupied the White House. Other environmental conditions may influence Presidents' legislative success: elections and public opinion, timing, party control of Congress, and partisan leadership in Congress. Party control of the White House provided some explanatory power, as did selected years in terms of office and Presidents individually.

Presidents have very little control over many of these conditions, which limits their ability to affect the outcome. Although all of the conditions are potentially useful in explaining Presidential success, we posit policy areas as among the most important influences.

Functional policy areas revealed substantial differences in congressional approval. Distributive policies exhibited the greatest success, followed by redistributive, and then regulatory policies. Eisenhower is the only President for whom this ordering does not apply. Surprisingly, distributive policy is the area where there were greatest partisan differences in success, perhaps because subsidy issues can be very ideological and also because Democrats emphasize such group benefits (Pomper 1980, 146-47). Distributive policies were approved more frequently during Presidents' first year in office and least frequently during their last. Overall, distributive policy reveals greatest Congressional deference to Presidents' initiatives.

Regulatory policies obtained the lowest level of approval overall, perhaps corresponding with increased Presidential control efforts. The regulatory realm produced the fewest partisan differences, and as with distributive policies, more initiatives were approved during first years and least during last years in office. Clearly, regulation was the policy area receiving the greatest Congressional inspection, if not outright dominance—scrutiny that has increased especially since Nixon.

Presidents were not as dominant in the redistributive realm as expected. Their efforts were only moderately successful, and beginning in 1973, Congress became more assertive. Although partisan differences appeared, differences in success for selected years did not materialize for redistributive issues.

The functional typology seems to have worked better than the substantive one for this chapter, but the question arises of how well the six substantive areas reflect the functional (Lowi) typology. For success, the fit is quite imperfect; indeed, the two substantive areas in each functional category performed vastly differently overall and on the environmental variables. Thus, even our typical examples of functional areas raise doubts about any claim of rough equivalence between functional and substantive policy.

While the substantive issue-areas seem more controversial than domestic policy overall, success was somewhat higher for the former and with the six areas aggregated. Poverty initiatives obtained greatest success and antitrust initiatives the least. An overview of the dominant environmental conditions employed illustrates their discriminating power on Congressional success. Differences were evident among the individual Presidents. Johnson was the only President to attain adoption of over half of his initiatives overall, while Ford received less than one-third. Eisenhower did better than the other two Republicans and even better overall than Kennedy, who scored much worse on this measure of Presidential-Congressional relations than he had on support (modification).

It should not be surprising that Democrats did better than Republicans overall and in every functional and substantive policy area except price supports (due largely to Eisenhower's high success). Party of the President produced some surprises, however: greatest party differences on distributive policy; no partisan differences on civil rights or either of the subissue areas (water projects or school desegregation).

Selected years also had some discriminating value. For example, they fit the functional areas (except redistributive) better than party differences, which usually varied within functional policy areas. Overall, Presidents were more successful during reelection years and least during first years for both functional and substantive areas of public policy.

What has this examination of Congressional success revealed? The President influences Congressional decisions only marginally in domestic policy. In turn, many factors affect Congressional support for his legislative positions and the success of his policy initiatives. He gets his way earlier rather than later in his Administration and also more frequently when he rallies his partisans and utilizes Congressional leaders in policy formulation. Other factors also influence success. Presidential leadership over Congress is increasingly difficult in the domestic realm, however; conflict rather than cooperation has been more the norm in recent years. This chapter has shown that Congress is not exalted in domestic policy formation, but neither is the President. Congress plays its greatest role in policy adoption, and if seldom capable of innovation, it certainly can thwart Presidential initiatives should it so desire.

NOTES

1. As might be expected, there is a difference of opinion about what concept is measured by these indicators. Some authors allude to power (Wildavsky 1966; Peppers 1975; Sigelman 1979); others to influence (Edwards 1980; Sigelman 1979, 1198); and still others to Presidential relations with Congress (LeLoup and Shull 1979b). Because these concepts continue to remain ambiguous after years of scholars' wrestling with them, they are simply used interchangeably in this analysis.

2. The support score is the average of the House and Senate approval percentages.

3. The observed decline in support for Presidents over time squares with Mueller's finding that Presidents lose support from their "coalition of minorities" (1973). Kennedy is the only exception to this declining support during last year, and surely no one would have predicted the abrupt end to his Administration.

4. A possible explanation is that resource policies have political payoff for Congressmen, and therefore, they prefer their own initiatives to those of the President.

5. This is probably due to the fact that these issues started as redistributive and still have redistributive elements.

6. Cramer's $V = 0.16$ after adjusting for boundedness (chi square significant above .001 level).

7. Discussion of the Carter-Reagan experience may be found in other chapters.

8. The extent to which Congress actually can (or does) lead the President in domestic policy formation is explored in Chapters 6-7.

Summary and
Conclusion   6

This book has made a case for the importance of policy process, regardless of the terms particular scholars have chosen to describe the various stages. Policy content is also important. Functional and substantive areas help explain the phenomena observed here and seem to have empirical as well as theoretical utility. Finally, elected political actors can also make a difference in domestic policy formation. Their influence across the stages and areas of policy are summarized here; actor roles are addressed in greater depth in Chapter 7.

CHANGING POLICY PROCESS

The policy formation process occurs in sequential steps or stages. The advantages of looking at policy in this way were explained in Chapter 1. Writers have found policy cycles useful in predicting Presidential policy leadership (Shank 1980; Shull 1979a). Policy stages emphasize the cyclical and fluid nature of the process, as well as interaction among actors. We have found in this book considerable relationship between stages and actors; that is, actor influence varies substantially across policy stages.

Actors and the Policy Process

Presidents use agenda-setting to assert their leadership. An increasing use of rhetoric suggests that they recognize the importance of agenda advocacy. Those Presidents who actively articulate an agenda of items they perceive to be important have more support and success later. Early advocacy and assertiveness do have some payoff, but Presidents must make difficult initial choices. Some positions on issues are innovative or controversial, or both, and the longer a program remains on the agenda, the more likely opposition will emerge in Congress. As Light (1982, 218) succinctly states, the President must "move it or lose it."

The practically unlimited latitude Presidents have to articulate an agenda becomes more constrained as early as policy initiation. Presidents can define a problem but cannot easily control a situation. Here choices must be carefully considered as the agenda becomes more defined. Generally, more rhetorical Presidents are also the ones who formally initiate more policy requests. Policy initiatives tell us a lot about Presidential leadership. Presidents made more requests of Congress through the 1960s. A decline ensued under Nixon and Ford; then Presidential activism in policy initiation resumed under Carter and Reagan.

Policy modification provides an important opportunity for Congress to assess Presidential statements and actions. Presidents have not, over time, taken more positions on legislative votes, and modification by Congress generally is low. Claims of a more aggressive Congress (for example, Sundquist 1981) do not hold up in our measures of modification. Despite a fair amount of conflict of various kinds over legislative votes on which Presidents take positions, Congress normally accedes to Presidential wishes. This finding suggests a green light for the assertive President. He has the ability to take positions on legislative initiatives with little fear of repudiation.

There is no doubt that Congress has the last word on policy adoption, and here much greater legislative assertiveness over time is evident. Congress disapproves a rather high proportion of Presidential initiatives (regardless of Presidential assertiveness); Congressional disapproval has been increasing. The claims of Congressional resurgence have greater validity in policy adoption (Sundquist 1981). Congress may even be capable of innovation, or at least leadership, such as during May 1982 when it rewrote the discredited initial 1983 Reagan budget. Some of the potential for legislative leadership will be explored in Chapter 7.

Conditions Affecting Actor Discretion

Several circumstances influence the degree of Presidential and Congressional influence in the process of domestic policy formation.[1] Three of the most important variables hypothesized here are individual Presidents, political party differences, and selected years in Presidents' terms of office.

Presidents Individually

In summarizing the empirical findings of this research, Table 6-1 allows us to compare the level of activity of Presidents in the policy process overall. Activity is certainly one component of leadership. Johnson (and Franklin Roosevelt, for whom comparable data are not available) are ranked at the top in terms of providing strong leadership over Congress, but both Presidents had huge partisan majorities to guarantee support for their programs. Both Presidents, however, asked for so much that eventually their relations with Congress deteriorated.

The weakest Congressional leader based upon the empirical data is Ford (see Table 6-1). When Ford took office in August 1974, he stated that he wanted not a honeymoon but a good marriage with

Table 6-1. Presidential

President		Agenda-Setting		Initiation	Policy Stage
		(attn./yr.)	(support,%)	(#/yr.)	Modification (#positions/yr.)
Eisenhower	N	51	61	53	130
	rank	6	4	3	6
Kennedy	N	97	96	112	187
	rank	3	1	2	3
Johnson	N	104	91	149	242
	rank	2	2	1	1.5
Nixon	N	73	52	42	171
	rank	5	5	4	4
Ford	N	79	35	29	163
	rank	4	6	5	5
Carter	N	112	63	___[a]	242
	rank	1	3		1.5

Note: Scores based upon six substantive areas.

Congress. He got neither. He ascended to the office at a time when Congress was attempting to regain the authority that most of its members felt had been too easily given or grabbed by a succession of Presidents. This, plus the huge opposition party control, made it difficult for him (or perhaps any other recent President) to assert dynamic Congressional leadership. Nixon also qualifies as a weak legislative leader. He appears to have paid the least attention of any recent President to Congress, and thus, it is somewhat bewildering that he got his way as often as he did.

All other Presidents to varying degrees fall between these extremes. Reagan was surprisingly assertive, but it is still too early to predict his leadership capacity. Carter had poor Congressional relations despite large partisan majorities in Congress and substantial activity (see Table 6-1). Kennedy was the first President in over fifty years whose coattails were too short to make gains for his party in Congress by his initial election. Although it was not due to lack of will, Kennedy was unable to get his programs passed. His

Activity in the Policy Process

Policy Stage		Totals		
Modification (support,%)	Adoption (%approved)	Score/observ.	X score	Overall rank
71	43	25/6	4.2	4
4	2			
85	41	13/6	2.2	3
1	3			
77	57	10/6	1.7	1
2.5	1			
64	37	27/6	4.5	5
5	4			
58	30	31/6	5.2	6
6	5			
77	—[a]	8/4	2.0	2
2.5				

a. Data unavailable after 1975.

success was little better than that of Nixon or Ford, who suffered from overwhelming partisan opposition in Congress. The ranking for Eisenhower (Table 6-1) is unusually high, given common perceptions of his passivity. His bipartisan style may have helped his Congressional relations.

The rankings in Table 6-1 reveal that all Democrats were more active than all Republicans. Reagan may be the exception, but the importance of party is clearly demonstrated by this research. Party and selected years in Presidential terms also distinguished actor roles in the policy formation process.

Party

Table 6-2 summarizes Presidential and Congressional assertiveness overall, by political party, and by selected years in Presidential terms. Democrats emerge as more assertive and expansive than Republicans across the policy formation process. While some of the Republicans tried to be contractive, Reagan is the only recent President who sought (and partially achieved) major reductions in the domestic sphere. Virtually no party differences were evident in the amount of Presidential rhetoric in agenda-setting. Greater party differences occurred in the later substages (see Table 6-2). Democrats made far more requests on a yearly basis than did Republicans. Also, although Democrats took more positions on legislative votes, and frequently generated conflict in Congress, they still received much greater support (and less modification) overall. Finally, Democrats also obtain adoption of more of their initiatives than do Republican Presidents.

Year

Expansion and activity in agenda-setting occur more frequently during Presidents' first year in office. Although more rhetoric is produced during first years (see Table 6-2), inexperience and confusion may abound (Light 1982, 44). Fewer initiatives are made during first years, and there is greater Congressional deference then (in modification). While Presidents are again quite assertive during last years, they lose a large amount of their political capital and receive the least Congressional support then. Presidents are least assertive and expansive during reelection years, and although that is when Congress most often challenges Presidential initiatives, there was little difference in policy adoption by selected years in office (see Table 6-2).

Assessment

What can be concluded about the roles and influence of Congress and the President in domestic policy formation? The hypothesized influence of these actors seems to hold: Presidents exert greater influence in the earlier stages of the policy process (agenda-setting and initiation), but the influence of Congress is greater near the end (modification and adoption). Congress does seem to defer to the President until later in policymaking, when its prerogatives become more influential. Agenda-setting and initiation show how important it is to try, but modification and, particularly, adoption reveal how hard it is for Presidents to attain their goals. Thus, Presidential statements and actions contribute only minimally to Congressional support and success. Nevertheless, the cyclical nature of policy is revealed when we observe legislative adoption influencing the size and composition of the subsequent Presidential agenda.

Policy process was the primary dependent variable of this research. Roles of actors and policy types varied considerably across stages of policy formation, encouraging fluidity in the policy process. Although each stage revealed quite different interaction patterns, overlap occurred because there is not perfect division among them. Environmental conditions accounted for some of the differences observed in influence. Democrats are more assertive but also obtain greater support for their policies than do Republicans. Rhetoric by Presidents during their first years in office is not followed by greater action, although it should be because of Congressional deference to the President in the honeymoon period.

CHANGING POLICY CONTENT: FUNCTIONAL AREAS

This book considers policy areas the most important contextual constraint on the policy formation process. A number of writers have identified the conceptual and empirical utility of looking at policy according to functional and substantive areas. Parallel findings in the executive and legislative branches lend credibility to the belief that elected officials think in policy terms. In an effort to reduce a large number of decisions to more manageable choices, officials tend to perceive and categorize policy similarly into policy areas. But does the content of policy predict (or even explain) actor

Table 6-2. Presidential-Congressional Assertiveness

	Agenda-Setting	Initiation	Modification	Adoption
Overall				
President	Higher	Moderately High	Moderately Low	Lower
Congress	Lower	Moderately Low	Moderately High	Higher
Party				
Democrats	No Difference	Higher	Higher	Higher
Republicans	No Difference	Lower	Lower	Lower
Year				
First	Higher	Lower	Higher	Moderately Lower [a]
Last	Moderate	Higher	Lower	Moderate [a]
Reelection	Lower	Moderate	Moderately Higher	Moderately Higher [a]

a. No significant differences by selected years

roles and behavior? If policy areas are more important than, say, Presidents, we must be able to show that variations by policy areas are greater than variations among individual Presidents. In order to see if areas are the most important determinants of the policy process, the data are broken down according to functional and substantive areas of public policy.

Overview of Functional Areas

This study found empirical distinctions among the three components of the Lowi typology to complement the theoretical distinctions many have claimed for it. It was observed to have discriminating value, just as have substantive typologies of Presidential initiatives to Congress. It differentiated among distributive, regulatory, and redistributive initiatives overall, by Presidents individually, by political party, and across time (by selected years). We shall now review the importance of these variables for understanding the process of policy formation.

Presidents were posited as interested in redistributive policies and Congress as interested in distributive and regulatory issues. Some support for this expectation occurred in Presidential agenda-setting, where by far the most Presidential rhetoric appeared on redistributive issues.[2] Presidents initiated the most on distributive policies, however, and that is also where they received their least conflict but greatest adoption (success) (see Table 6-3). Overall, regulatory issues fare most poorly in Presidential assertiveness and legislative adoption, but a decided growth in this policy area is taking place. Redistributive issues were subject to greatest modification, and therefore Presidential leadership was less effective on this policy area than had been expected. Indeed, greater conflict now arises in all three policy areas than in the past. These differences in the policy process frequently are magnified when we examine the environmental variables.

Conditions Affecting Actor Discretion

Presidents Individually

Substantial differences among the Presidents are evident when policy is disaggregated into functional areas. Eisenhower was the

Table 6-3. Functional Areas in the Policy Process (by Environmental Variables)

	Agenda-Setting (# items)	Initiation (proportion)	Modification (#votes/yr— controversy)	Adoption (percent approved)
Overall				
D	Moderate	Higher	Lower	Higher
G	Lower	Lower	Moderate	Lower
R	Higher	Moderate	Higher	Moderate
Party				
Dems.				
D	Mod. Higher	Higher	Lower	Higher
G	Lower	Lower	Moderate	Lower
R	Higher	Moderate	Higher	Moderate
Reps.				
D	Moderate	Higher	Lower	Higher
G	Lower	Moderate	Moderate	Moderate
R	Higher	Moderate	Higher	Moderate

148

Selected Year

First			
D	Moderate	Higher	Higher
G	Lower	Lower	Lower
R	Higher	Moderate	Moderate
Last			
D	Moderate	Higher	Higher
G	Lower	Moderate	Moderate
R	Higher	Lower	Moderate
Reelection			
D	Moderate	Higher	Higher
G	Lower	Lower	Lower
R	Higher	Moderate	Moderate

Note: D = distributive
G = regulatory
R = redistributive
a. Data on modification not available for
   specified years.

least rhetorical President in all policy areas (see Table 6-4). He did emphasize redistributive initiatives relatively more than most other Presidents. He took few positions on legislative votes and received considerable success on his initiatives. Eisenhower obtained greater approval of his regulatory requests than any other President.

Kennedy's realm of greatest rhetoric was in foreign policy. He cared little for regulatory issues. He generated substantial conflict in all policy areas, and thus his overall success was quite low, particularly for a Democrat.

Far more than Kennedy, Johnson's rhetoric emphasized domestic issues (see Table 6-4). As a pragmatic politician, he especially initiated distributive issues, but he also did exceedingly well in obtaining approval for his redistributive proposals, despite their ground-breaking character.

The emphasis shifted under Nixon and Ford as regulatory issues became the most dominant. Neither President got more than a third of his requests approved in any policy area. Ford was particularly unsuccessful in the regulatory area, which had become extremely important to him (see Table 6-4).

Despite the positive results of many regulatory policies of the 1960s and 1970s, a backlash against government regulation occurred under Carter and Reagan. What began as deregulation under Carter became a definite decline of enforcement effort under Reagan (Chelf 1981, 271). Both Presidents continued the deemphasis on distributive policies, and certainly Reagan's interest and activity in redistribution run counter to that pursued by his Republican predecessors.

Party

Democratic Presidents clearly devote most of their rhetoric and actions to distributive and redistributive policies; Republicans give greater attention to regulation (see Table 6-3). This finding squares with Kessel's notion of greater Republican concern for economic-regulatory factors (1977, 428). However, the partisan differences on redistributive issues were less than anticipated; indeed, distributive issues proved most partisan. Closer to expectations, distributive issues were least controversial and redistributive issues most controversial. Regulatory issues were least often approved by Congress, especially for Democrats.

Year

Selected years were not particularly discriminating by functional areas across the stages of policy formation. First years in office appear to be more innovative, and reelection years are least innovative. Regulatory issues are initiated least often by Presidents (particularly during first and reelection years), and also adopted least often (particularly during first years). Although redistributive items appeared most often in presidential rhetoric (see Table 6-3), Presidents initiated a higher proportion of distributive ones, especially during last and reelection years. But these two selected years (last and reelection) are when Presidents' distributive initiatives are most likely to be rejected by Congress.

Assessment

How close do these findings meet our expectations? Distributive issues were more stable and usually the least conflictual or visible of the three functional policy areas. All actors get a piece of the action, and whatever changes do occur are likely to be gradual (incremental). Regulatory policies came of age by the late 1960s. Such issues became a more important proportion of the domestic policy arena due to increased complexity of policymaking and the need for social regulation. Redistributive policies generate the most conflict and visibility and perhaps, therefore, the least stability among the three policy areas. It is also the area where innovative, nonincremental change is most likely to occur. Yet there were numerous surprises in the examination of functional policy areas, such as the high salience and partisanship of distributive policy.

Time was observed to be an important influence on the Lowi functional typology. As regulatory policy became more prominent in Presidential proposals, a corresponding decline had to appear elsewhere. It did not come from the popular and immensely stable distributive area but logically from the area of greatest conflict—redistribution. Regulatory policy may result in some redistribution, however. The observed long-term decline in redistributive initiatives confirms the assertion by Ripley and Franklin of diminishing group and governmental support for that activity (1980, 156). Despite the importance of time, there were differences by individual Presidents, party, and selected years in office.

Table 6-4. Functional Areas in the Policy Process (by President)

	Agenda-Setting (# items)	Initiation (Proportion)	Modification (# votes/yr-controversy)	Adoption (percent approved)
Eisenhower				
D	22	41	4	48
G	7	22	13	49
R	110	37	18	38
Kennedy				
D	130	45	15	45
G	13	5	7	31
R	227	40	36	34

Johnson				
D	153	45	9	65
G	29	28	37	44
R	211	27	37	64
Nixon				
D	56	37	14	34
G	20	42	24	26
R	139	21	28	30
Ford				
D	137	31		33
G	36	47	a	20
R	135	23		33

Note: D = Distributive

G = Regulatory

R = Redistributive

a. Date unavailable.

Explaining Actor Roles

Adopting Lowi's preferred use of the typology as an independent variable predicting politics, Congress was found to disapprove a relatively high proportion of initiatives, particularly in the increasingly important regulatory area. For whatever reason, Congress is playing a more important role in policy formation than previously.[3] This finding has major implications for Presidential-Congressional relations. Presidents possibly would achieve greater success were they to involve Congress in an early and active role in agenda-setting. So far, Presidents have not gravitated toward this type of shared power.

Congress carefully scrutinized the Nixon-Ford cutbacks in redistributive policies. It was clearly more progressive than the President on social programs after 1969 (Orfield 1975, 187, 225). Many redistributive issues like civil rights (especially school desegregation), unemployment, and tax policy moved more into the province of Congress—certainly after 1972. Distributive and regulatory policies also came in for increasing legislative review and subsequent disapproval.

It may be less the case in the future that social policy is the area of greatest conflict. Regulatory policy became the more conflictual policy area beginning in the 1970s. This greater tension may be due to both actors' having a moderate degree of discretion in regulation. It was not the primary interest of either Congress or the President. At the same time, it was the area of growth, counterbalanced by a relative decline in both distributive and redistributive policy. Because most regulations are promulgated by the bureaucracy—often by independent agencies with only limited Presidential control—Congress may continue to cultivate its frequently symbiotic relations with such agencies, further frustrating the President in policy formation.

Utility of Functional Areas

Functional policy areas aid in understanding actor roles and behavior. The Lowi typology provided several advantages for this study of policy formation. It provided order and coherence; it enhanced generalizability (by moving away from the case method and reducing the unwieldiness—5,716 cases overall and upward of 470 yearly); it helped identify actor emphasis; and it aided in theoretical development toward understanding these emphases and relations in policy formation.

Like others who have attempted real-world classification based upon the typology, however, classifying policies in the scheme can be difficult and frustrating. The issues may change their designation over time, and uncertainty persists over whether the three categories can be made mutually exclusive. Despite Lowi's important contribution to the policy literature, empirical investigations continue to reveal cracks (if not large holes) in the "theory". Continual development of the typology inevitably complicates the original, overly simplistic formulation.

Lowi's typology has been considered "not testable because the basic concepts are not operationalizable" (Greenberg et al. 1977, 1536). This book has tried to define the concepts more explicitly and has identified issues that fit somewhat in each category (see Appendix). Some differences in Presidential and Congressional attention and behavior were observed generally along lines anticipated by the "theory," but the conclusions have, of necessity, been tentative. We still cannot be certain of Lowi's claim that policymakers perceive inherent differences in these policies. There is somewhat better evidence of such perceptions in substantive areas of policy.

CHANGING POLICY CONTENT: SUBSTANTIVE AREAS

Although functional areas were useful in this research, substantive areas demonstrated even greater power to explain the policy process. We have discussed the imperfect correspondence between substantive and functional policy areas. A summary of where we place the six substantive areas of this study in conjunction with the five Clausen-Kessel areas and the three functional (Lowi) areas may be seen in Figure 6-1. The figure is not designed to show precisely where policy areas fall but to indicate the mix of distribution, regulation, and redistribution that most substantive issues have. Thus a continuum seemed more useful than discrete categories. Note that policy areas move generally from public works as the most distributive to poverty as the most redistributive. Some issues are, of course, broader in their scope than others, as the impressionistic lines in Figure 6-1 suggest. The impact of price

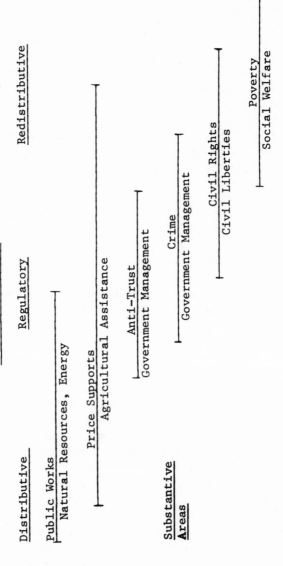

Figure 6-1. Relation of Functional and Substantive Policy Areas

Functional Areas

Distributive   Regulatory   Redistributive

Public Works
Natural Resources, Energy

Price Supports
Agricultural Assistance

Anti-Trust
Government Management

Crime
Government Management

Civil Rights
Civil Liberties

Poverty
Social Welfare

Substantive
Areas

supports, for example, can range from distributive to redistributive, while the impact of antitrust usually is narrowly regulatory.

We now review changes in the content of these six issue-areas across the policy process overall and by individual Presidents. Then we examine change by political party and by selected years in Presidential terms of office.

Summary of Changing Content

The substance of the six policy areas revealed considerable change across time and the policy process. Generally the issue-areas were more salient than domestic policy overall or the three functional areas. Also, a broadening of the scope of governmental intervention was observed over time in virtually all six policy areas.

Price Supports

Price supports was a controversial distributive issue-area and an important component of agricultural policy during the period studied. A topic that became increasingly significant (particularly with Kennedy) through Johnson, it then diminished in Presidential attention. The issue-area reemerged as more significant to later Presidents. No unified policy was established, perhaps because of disunity among clientele groups, and we began to see calls for reductions in the role of government in this policy area by the early 1970s. Although all Presidents seem to have preferred the marketplace for setting agricultural prices, Democrats were more tolerant of government intervention. Presidents continually sought to gain control over price supports by such tactics as requesting greater discretion for the Secretary of Agriculture, usually unsuccessfully. These Presidents either could not or would not wean government away from policies of subsidizing agricultural production.

The price supports issue-area revealed a move away from support for specific commodities toward loans for farmers themselves. By the 1970s, subsidies had been reduced on many commodities, a phenomenon increasingly supported by both Congress and Presidents. Price supports remains an area where Congress wishes to assert its prerogatives.

Public Works

Change in the substantive character of public works was also evident. Attention moved away from highways toward mass transit; increased interest (with the exception of Carter) in nuclear development through the Reagan Administration; intensified concern for federal parks; and changed emphasis in water projects toward pollution, waste, and environmental issues.[4] More general programs like airports and parks became more important, but also more controversial, by the mid-1970s. Two popular programs, urban mass transit and aid to the financially troubled railway industry, were nearly always upheld in Congress.

We focused special attention on water projects as a major (largest) distributive component of public works policy. The sub-issue began to shift away from recreation projects to the more regulatory issues of water conservation and protection. Nevertheless, the pork barrel dimension remained as both Carter and Reagan were forced to accept more water projects than they wanted. In contrast to the other distributive area, the public works clientele was more unified.

Crime

As the only issue-area where overwhelmingly nonsupportive sentiments were expressed, crime also received growing Presidential attention except by Carter. Drug abuse, rioting, and handgun controls were weighty issues in the late 1960s and early 1970s. The more humane emphasis in the 1960s on prevention and protection for the accused gave way in the 1970s to stricter penalties and separating criminals from the rest of society. However, these seemingly more repressive policies after 1973 by Nixon, Ford, and Reagan were not supported by a Democratic Congress.

The crime issue-area broadened over the years. A larger array of issues occurred under Johnson and Nixon than previously or since that time. While more traditional crime issues appeared (such as restoring the death penalty for certain federal crimes, detention and release questions), broader civil liberties issues also began to emerge (such as making it a crime to riot, have an abortion, or use children in pornography). Some crime issues changed very little. Concern for internal security, for example, remained for twenty years but shifted from communists under Eisenhower to student rioters and war protesters under Johnson and Nixon.

Antitrust

Antitrust was the least salient policy area, but it too experienced steady growth in federal enforcement powers throughout this period. After taking a hands-off position in antitrust during the 1950s, Congress became more activist in desiring to regulate business in the 1960s. The issue-area, however, was not particularly salient to Presidents or to Congress. Many of the subissues were relatively routine, dealing with mergers and damages to be paid for law violations. Congress began to relax its strictness by the mid-1970s; for example, it allowed exemptions from antitrust provisions for railroads and energy producers. Antitrust is becoming more salient, however, as competition in American industry continues to decline and as challenges to FTC regulations persist (Katzmann 1981).

Civil Rights

All Presidents made general statements about the desirability of equal opportunity, but civil rights now seems a less pressing issue-area than in the late 1950s and 1960s. Concern moved away from electoral equality, as advocated policies succeeded, toward the more sensitive equality of housing and education. Education was the largest subissue, with desegregation being the most controversial problem, especially the advisability of mandatory busing to achieve racial balance. By 1970 there was general retrenchment in Presidential civil rights advocacy. The Nixon and Ford approach was to encourage rather than force compliance. After a brief respite under Carter, that approach seems to have resumed in the early 1980s. Even the controversial issue of school desegregation diminished in importance, perhaps because no recent President or Congress supported court-ordered busing. Upon the diminution in salience of school desegregation, civil rights efforts moved forward in public accommodations and housing, the latter proving most controversial and persistent. Perhaps unwittingly, Reagan's conservative actions have returned civil rights to a prominent place on the public policy agenda (LeLoup and Shull 1982).

Poverty

Poverty proved a broad issue-area; almost as encompassing as the social welfare dimension studied by other researchers. Employ-

Table 6-5. Substantive

| Policy Area | Agenda-Setting | | Policy Stage Initiation |
	(Attention/yr.)	(Support,%)	(#/yr)
Price Supports (N)	6.4	42	6.8
rank	5	4	4
Public Works (N)	18.4	70	31.7
rank	2	3	1
Crime (N)	5.5	9	10.2
rank	4	6	3
Anti-Trust (N)	2.5	33	1.8
rank	6	5	6
Civil Rights (N)	15.8	88	5.3
rank	3	1	5
Poverty (N)	31.1	78	21.3
rank	1	2	2
Totals	N=79.7	X̄=69	N=77.1

ment was always a major subissue, as were education and health. Among the more salient poverty subissues were Head Start, school lunches, day care, and particularly, unemployment compensation (throughout the period), job training (after the mid-1960s), and food stamps (in the 1970s). Food stamps became quite controversial, with numerous amendments regarding eligibility of students, strikers, and other recipients. In the subissue of housing, there was a move away from public housing toward various types of direct aid to poor or unemployed renters and home owners. Housing was not a large subset of poverty but continued to remain salient throughout the time period. Since the early 1970s, subsidized housing has become the third largest welfare program, behind Medicaid and food stamps. Republican Presidents through Reagan generally sought cuts in existing programs and particularly wished to move away from subsidized housing units.

Areas in the Policy Process

Policy Stage Modification (# positions/yr)	(Support, %)	Adoption (% approved)	Totals (Score/observations)	X̄ score	Rank
5.0	64	53	24/6	4.0	4.5
4	5	2			
7.0	60	50	17/6	2.8	2
2	6	3			
1.3	78	41	24/6	4.0	4.5
5	2	4			
.3	71	24	33/6	5.5	6
6	4	6			
6.5	86	33	18/6	3.0	3
3	1	5			
8.3	73	62	10/6	1.7	1
1	3	1			
N=28.4	X̄ = 73	X̄=50	126/36	3.5	-

Overview of Substantive Areas

Presidents gave greatest agenda attention to poverty and least to antitrust (see Table 6-5), although the importance of the latter area began to increase and price supports began to decline. With the exception of crime, Presidents also were supportive in their policy statements of these issue-areas, particularly civil rights. Excluding civil rights, these tendencies were also evident in policy initiation. Presidential assertiveness on civil rights was supported to a surprisingly high degree by Congress; indeed, a higher proportion of their positions were supported (that is, not modified) there than on any other policy area (see Table 6-5). Civil rights positions were seldom modified because they were also rarely adopted. Poverty initiatives were approved most often, but only one-third of civil rights initiatives were approved. This last statement also summarizes the six policy areas across the four stages of policy formation.

Overall, poverty attained the greatest attention and support from Presidents and Congress and antitrust the least (see Table 6-5). The generally noncontroversial public works ranked second, and the presumed (but not actually) controversial civil rights scored a strong third overall.

Conditions Affecting Actor Discretion

Presidents Individually

Ironically, two of the least rhetorical Presidents, Eisenhower and Ford, had much to say about the generally nonsalient issue-area of antitrust. Eisenhower gave relatively little attention, however, to such policy areas as crime, public works, and poverty. Although he was not very assertive, Eisenhower fared better with Congress than any of his Republican successors. He was the only Republican President until Reagan to have, however briefly, a Republican Congress.

Although neither Eisenhower nor Kennedy requested much in the civil rights area, the latter's success was surprisingly low. He was totally uninterested in crime but much more assertive than Eisenhower had been on price supports and poverty. If Eisenhower did well with Congress for a Republican, Kennedy's performance was poor for a Democrat. Even in the crime issue-area, Kennedy had little success on requests for drug legislation.

Johnson's activity and Congressional relations were the most consistent of any other President. He usually took the most frequent and intense positions, particularly on civil rights and public works. Yet on this latter issue-area, even he could not establish fees for users of the public waterways or greater executive control over the funding of such projects.

Nixon and Ford exhibited similarities. Both took quite intense positions on crime issues. Both pushed for stricter penalties and for greater enforcement of existing laws against crime generally. Nixon also seems to have had little interest in civil rights. High support for Nixon's stance on busing was symptomatic of growing Congressional conservatism on the issue-area.

The greater scrutiny given by Presidents since Ford to public works and antitrust demonstrates their growing importance in the policy process. Ford was the first recent President to express considerable rhetoric on antitrust and also the first to back away from strict government enforcement. Ford offered relatively few initiatives on the two distributive issue-areas (price supports and public works) and was quite unsuccessful on most policy areas.

Carter demonstrated more rhetoric on a yearly basis than any other President. He was particularly assertive on public works, but there is no evidence that either his or Reagan's efforts were very effective. Legislative conflict was minimal, except on civil rights, where Congress modified more of his positions than those of any other President. Certainly this is one issue-area where Congress took the more conservative positions. Carter received low support for his price supports positions, but his poverty positions were more favorably received. Carter was rarely interested in distributive issues but much more so in regulation (deregulation particularly) than most Democrats.

Reagan's desire to make cuts throughout the domestic realm led him to concentrate on redistributive issues. He charged in September 1982 that the poor "would be appreciably better off today if the Great Society had never occurred. . . . [It ate] away at the underpinnings to the free enterprise system . . . [and] brought economic progress of the poor to a halt" (*New Orleans Times-Picayune States Item*, 9/16/82, 1). All Presidents except Reagan supported broader coverage and increased benefits for the unemployed. Republicans stressed job training, the elimination of Aid for Dependent Children, and budget cuts in such benefits and services. It seems ironic that CETA, advocated strongly by Nixon, Ford, and Carter, was among the first programs targeted for elimination by Reagan. Reagan also greatly contracted the civil rights policies of the previous generation (LeLoup and Shull 1982). Even more than Carter, he was interested in government deregulation. Reagan fared worse with Congress in his contractive proposals in these policy areas after 1981 than he did during his successful honeymoon year.

Party

Democrats paid greater attention to all issue-areas but crime and in their policy statements provided greater support than Republicans to all policy areas. Republicans increasingly were nonsupportive, with more specific statements focusing on self-help, fiscal conservatism, work requirements for aid, and program decentralization. (Illustrative of the latter is Reagan's stated desire to turn welfare programs back to the states.) The two regulatory issue-areas illustrate considerable party differences: crime least partisan and antitrust most partisan. Republicans through Ford were actually more supportive than Democrats of efforts to expand the roles of the FTC and the Anti-Trust Division of the Justice Department. Carter and Reagan, however, were more reflective of the partisan differences expected on antitrust policy. Some partisan differences also emerged on public works, such as when Republicans deemphasized the federal role or when Democrats tried to make generally distributive programs more redistributive by emphasizing the employment and redevelopment potential of public works.

If Democratic rhetoric was greater than that of Republicans, so were their overall actions more frequent (initiatives and positions on legislative votes). Again the anomaly is antitrust. Democrats obtain far less modification but greater adoption overall than Republicans. This latter success is magnified in antitrust and poverty.

Year

Presidents offer greater support in their policy statements during their last year in office for every issue-area but crime. Perhaps because of its emotional nature, crime is supported by Presidents least during reelection years. Presidents also make fewer legislative requests during first years and most during their last years in office. All six substantive areas are emphasized more during Presidents' last years in office. Since most of these issue-areas are controversial, it stands to reason that Presidents choose such greater emphases when they are no longer politically vulnerable. A cynic might suggest that is the only time when they push controversy. Antitrust, the most extremely partisan of the six policy areas, receives greatest attention during reelection years, perhaps exacerbating party tensions. Similarly, in terms of amendments and number of votes, reelection years generate greater controversy (especially on price supports and civil rights) in Congress but least modification of Presidential positions. Also surprising, Presidents obtain little support during first years in office. Crime, civil rights, and poverty were adopted more during reelection years than in any other selected years in Presidential terms.

Assessment

Explaining Actor Roles

Most domestic programs exhibit a combination of executive and legislative leadership, although some policies traditionally have been dominated by one actor or the other. The following case studies provide examples of each type of actor influence.

President Dominant. The poverty program is the best known and perhaps the most extreme example of executive dominance in domestic policy initiation. Proposals were well underway before the Kennedy assassination but were solidified and reinforced by Johnson as he embraced poverty as his primary domestic concern (Donovan 1973, 26). Partly because the program had been developed almost exclusively by a White House task force, there was very little input by other actors. While Johnson wanted the administrative agency within the Executive Office so that he could protect the program, he was not very knowledgeable about the program's substance. As controversy over its provisions and the Vietnam war intensified, his personal interest in the poverty program waned.

Locating the Office of Economic Opportunity (OEO) within the Executive Office of the President made it easier for the less sympathetic Presidents, Nixon and Ford, to dismantle the program almost entirely. Even the more liberal Democrat Carter did not resurrect OEO. He instead advocated cutting the number of poverty programs, providing more direct assistance to the needy, and having the federal government administer the welfare system. Reagan was even more adamantly opposed to poverty programs, particularly the subissue of housing. Despite some Congressional support, the poverty realm remained mostly Presidential as lack of clientele pressures failed to inspire Congress.

Congress Dominant. Perhaps surprisingly, a larger number of the six issue-areas exhibit greater Congressional than Presidential leadership. The two distributive issues particularly fit this description. Congress has played a major role in farm policy since the 1950s and has sometimes initiated on its own (such as a 1975 bill to raise target prices on certain commodities). The fragmented agencies and goals (for example, conservation versus development) have kept public works within the domain of subgovernments and hence largely removed from Presidential leadership. Congress seldom deferred to recent Presidents on either of these distributive policy areas.

Another recent issue that is almost entirely initiated by Congress is criminal code reform. The complicated legislation recodifies federal criminal laws for the first time in the history of our nation, attempting to give order to a divergent body of law. The legislation is an example of the routine but complex measures that Congress frequently initiates. A coalition of liberals and conservatives in Congress compromised their differences and persuaded President Carter and Attorney General Griffin Bell to endorse their proposal. Yet after years of work, the measure has yet to pass Congress.

Mixed. Probably the most typical pattern is for a mixture of executive-legislative leadership. Where once Presidential leadership was important in both antitrust and civil rights, we now see much less White House dominance. "Old fashioned 'trust-busting' is now rare" (Anderson, Brady, and Bullock 1978, 209), and civil rights too is now much less a part of the Presidential agenda (Light 1982, 84).

Civil rights also reveals considerable movement from Presidential to Congressional initiation and back again. Nixon's southern strategy, his choice of Supreme Court nominees, and his opposition to busing all demonstrated a diminished concern for progressive civil rights policies. Carter reasserted executive leadership again in the area, not only in the United States but around the world. Reagan's indecisiveness in civil rights (moderate rhetoric but conservative actions) would seem to leave a void for Congress, but controversy within Congress prevents it from stepping into the leadership role.

Utility of Substantive Areas

We cannot say with certainty whether individual Presidents or substantive areas better predict or explain the policy process. A comparison of Tables 6-1 and 6-5 overall shows about the same variance among the six Presidents as among the six policy areas. Looking at the policy stages separately, however, policy areas invariably produced a greater range of values than did Presidents. Thus, policy areas demarcate the stages in the process better than do Presidents. The belief here is that the two working in conjunction provide even greater explanatory power. The substantive areas were definitely easier to classify than were functional areas, and they usually offer greater empirical validation.

But why is it necessary or desirable to incorporate functional or substantive typologies, or both, into policy research? A workable typology facilitates the identification of general principles better than case analysis since policies are grouped according to similar attributes. Such a procedure also aids in reducing the unwieldiness of considering a large number of policies separately, a problem that becomes more acute as the number of policies studied increases. Policy typologies are sometimes considered synonymous with categorizations or classifications, but a useful typology does more than merely simplify or provide order: it helps demonstrate the relation between process and content, such as the latter predicting the former (Lowi 1964; Steinberger 1980, 185); it adds an operational component with distinguishing variables, such as conflict or innovativeness; and it suggests inherent differences in the categories along such lines as participant roles or the relative impact of issues on target groups or society.

Briefly, typologies should allow the deduction of important hypotheses and also provide a "basis for stating conditions under which a given proposition is applicable" (Lowi 1972, 307). Lowi goes further in suggesting that his typology in particular will "convert phenomena into variables," "capture features of government that are politically significant," "build . . . toward whole models," and provide "the beginning of orderly control and prediction" (1972, 299, 307). Lowi is saying that typologies are theories, or at least greatly aid in developing theory. The lack of rigorous empirical tests has not yet allowed achievement of these goals. In just beginning this task, this book finds the functional typology more conceptually elegant but not as operationally useful as the substantive classification.

NOTES

1. Although the present focus is on the President, later sections of this chapter discuss Congress's role in policy formation.

2. Recall that surrogate categories were used for the functional typology in agenda-setting.

3. Dodd refers to the notion of policy cycles where periodic adjustments prevent either Congress or the President from acquiring too much power (1977, 299).

4. This increasingly regulatory component of public works was deleted in this research.

Toward Presidential-Congressional Partnership

Earlier chapters examined actor interactions across the stages and areas of public policy. We have finally arrived at the crucial question: so what? Does such interplay make any difference for the policy formation process, and how can we gauge the importance of these interactions? Now that we have summarized the findings of this research, we must ascertain what it all means. This chapter centers on the notion of leadership and whether and how policy goals can be furthered by cooperation between Congress and the President. The chapter ends with a look at the directions future research should take.

PRESIDENTIAL LEADERSHIP

Whether the President can exert leadership over Congress is related to many factors. His personality and popularity, the extent to which he seeks innovative change, the nature of the times and the timing of his proposals, the quality of his liaison staff, his previous experience, the extent to which he becomes personally involved, his skills (Edwards 1980), the degree of Congressional assertiveness, and the partisan and leadership composition of Congress may all be important. Some of these conditions seem interrelated, but there is no certain formula for strong versus weak leadership. The primary characteristic of a strong leader is effectiveness in obtaining desired results. Effort alone is not enough. Yet we believe the dimensions of activity (effort) and preferred role for government examined directly and indirectly throughout this book usually can be equated with effective leadership.

Presidents since the Depression have exhibited a wide range of activity. They have also differed considerably in whether they

advocate expansion (considerable increases) in government programs. Expansion is equated with liberalism and contraction and
the status quo with conservatism. There appears to be a positive
association between Presidential activism and the desire for
expansive policies. An impressionistic ranking of the Presidents on
these two variables is shown in Table 7-1, and a brief review
follows in order to substantiate the rankings.

Expansive

Most of Roosevelt's New Deal legislation passed during the first
one hundred days of 1933. It represented an unsurpassed flurry of
Presidential activity and expansion. Most of Roosevelt's social
programs probably would have been untenable in an earlier era not
plagued with the turmoil of the Great Depression. It is debatable
how revolutionary they were. Roosevelt did not adopt innovative
Keynesian economic policies, for example, and his policies proved
not up to the task of taking the country out of the Depression until
the U.S. involvement in World War II.

Next to Roosevelt, Johnson was the most active (and also
possibly the most expansionist) President in developing a legislative
program. Many of Johnson's Great Society programs were
holdovers from Kennedy's proposals that had not gotten off the
ground. At first, Johnson lacked any coherent policy of his own,
and few observers would have predicted from his past public
record that he would emerge as the champion of the disadvantaged.
Many of his programs were poorly conceived, however. He seemed
less interested in the substance of policy than in his determination
to achieve a national consensus. Nevertheless, Johnson asserted
himself personally and proposed quite innovative programs.

Contractive

At the opposite end of the activism spectrum from Roosevelt
stands Eisenhower, a President who initially believed that separa-
tion of powers meant he was to respond to legislative programs.
Eisenhower was subsequently advised by Congress that
Presidential action was expected, and, thereafter, his style became
more assertive. Yet he had a "reluctance to formulate goals or a

Table 7-1. Presidential Activity and Preferred Government Role

Preferred Govern- ment Role	Activity		
	Active	Mixed	Passive
Expansive	Roosevelt Johnson	Carter	-
Mixed	Kennedy	Truman	-
Contractive	Reagan[a,b]	Nixon	Ford[b] Eisenhower

a. Based on 1981.

b. Neither Ford nor Reagan squares with Barber's (1980) characteriza-
    tion of the former as active or the latter as passive.

distaste for those goals the demands of the system had thrust upon him" (Polsby 1976, 29). Given Eisenhower's conservatism and passivity, it is amazing that his few initiatives were not more contractive than they were.

Nixon's absorption with foreign policy allowed him little interest in domestic issues. He seemed vulnerable to convincing arguments without any overall plan, and there was general confusion about how domestic policy should be devised. Perhaps this lack of direction is one reason why the Administration's slogans, New Federalism or New American Revolution, never lasted. Nixon had no real policy, save retrenchment and program consolidation. Nixon did make new proposals (for example, wage and price controls and revenue sharing), so his domestic policies were not totally contractive. He even continued a number of Johnson's Great Society programs, if on a more limited basis.

Ford seems also best classified as a passive-contractive President, not in his relations with Congress but in his general dearth of new policy options.[1] He was criticized for slowness in developing new programs, which were "conservative in tone, and short on innovative break-throughs" (*National Journal*, 6/21/75, 928). Ford opposed expansive social programs, sought to trim government spending in many areas, and instituted numerous fiscal reforms. Ford, and especially Nixon, were both more active than Eisenhower but had poorer relations with Congress; the associations frequently were tense and even hostile (see Chapters 4-5).

Among the contraction-minded Presidents, Reagan was clearly the most active in pursuing his policy preferences (see Table 7-1). During his first year in office, Reagan was quite aggressive and politically effective against the disorganized Democrats in Congress in his push for reductions of long-standing liberal social programs. Contrary to predictions of passivity (Barber 1980), Reagan exerted forceful leadership in marked contrast to his predecessor, Jimmy Carter, who either could not or would not bury the hatchet with members of his own party in Congress. Reagan confounds the original expectation that Presidents who are active will also request expansive policies. Indeed, his activism (during 1981-82 at least) in a contractive direction was profound. Congress early on acceded to that change in direction. But sensing vulnerability by late 1981, it was much more assertive itself during 1982. Reagan's proposed

New Federalism, for example, was quickly discredited both in Congress and by governors. Also failing to be adopted were a host of conservative social programs.

Mixed

Truman, who thought himself an average man, had an average amount of expansionism and activity in domestic policy formation (see Table 7-1).[2] Perhaps at the time there was little that had not been tried under Roosevelt. Truman's Fair Deal was largely a holding pattern in the domestic arena in an effort to stave off an increasingly hostile Congress. Truman had neither the charm nor the support Roosevelt had. Nevertheless, he was the President who conceived and developed the idea of a formal legislative package from the Executive at the beginning of each session of Congress.

Contrary to popular mythology, Kennedy, although active in trying to formulate policy, was not very expansive (Ripley 1972, 6). While he may deserve some credit for Johnson's later successes, Kennedy's New Frontier presented a cautious approach to domestic policy. He generally ignored the issue of civil rights, but this appeal to southern conservatives in order to preserve party harmony was rarely effective. Although Kennedy reasserted the dynamism of the legislative President, particularly during his first year in office, little was initiated in the domestic area that could be termed expansionist. He was ineffective in obtaining proposals deviating from the status quo.

Carter developed a begrudging respect for Congress's prerogatives, a respect required of him and all future Presidents as Congress sheds its submissive ways and reasserts itself. Carter demonstrated personal assertiveness on some domestic issues, occasionally against the advice of some of his top advisers. He did not propose as many initiatives as had Roosevelt or Johnson, however, nor was he as supportive or as personally active (see Table 7-1). Although Carter's proposals were more expansive than those of his Republican predecessors, his inability to get more of them off the ground assured that his proposed slogan, a New Foundation, would not materialize. He was particularly weak in establishing priorities (Light 1982, 126; Davis 1979).

Assessment

These impressionistic comparisons are buttressed with the empirical findings of this research. It is, of course, much easier to measure activity than preference for government's role, and most of the measures used (see Table 6-1) primarily incorporate the former dimension. The support score under agenda-setting is somewhat analogous to liberalism and so may tap expansionism to some extent. What was observed in Table 6-1 generally confirms these impressionistic rankings, but limitations or unavailability of data, or both, ensure that perfect correspondence will not exist. If we equate activity and propensity for expansion with leadership, Johnson easily emerges as the President most exerting leadership over Congress, and Ford and Nixon emerge as the weakest Congressional leaders.

In domestic policy formation the power of the President in relation to Congress varies over time and issues. In the latter half of the twentieth century, Executive leadership over Congress has been expected, even by Congress. Even one of the most powerful Congressional leaders of all time, Lyndon Johnson, felt as a Congressman that only the President could initiate major legislation (Kearns 1976, 140). More than ever, Presidents are expected to lead, and most have at least attempted to do so. In spite of increased leadership powers, such as central clearance and legislative liaison, conditions must be right for a President's leadership to be accepted.

Presidents who have cooperated with Congress normally have had greater success with their programs, and, to a large measure, such cooperation is dependent upon the political climate. Each of the strong leaders had a partisan majority in Congress, while the Presidents who were weak leaders did not. Although it may not be essential to have a large or even a simple partisan majority, a philosophical working majority is necessary for the President's programs to pass and for support of his positions on legislative votes.

CONGRESSIONAL LEADERSHIP

Although Congress may be incapable of determining the nation's policy agenda by itself, it too can initiate policy. Congress is inclined toward initiation and innovation when a vacuum in Presidential leadership exists. If the President who would initiate policy is encouraged to cooperate with Congress, that body can be effective in collaboration with a strong President. Congress has strengthened its hand in many ways since Executive abuses during the Vietnam and Watergate eras. For every increase in Presidential leadership powers, there are corresponding Congressional checks. Yet genuine doubts exist about the competence of Congressional leadership.

If it is true that only the President can set policy priorities, then perhaps Congress is better off accepting certain elements of Presidential leadership, because cooperating with an energetic and effective President may even improve its own policy effectiveness. Certainly Congress was the most progressive of the three branches on social policy between 1969 and 1976. The time span is too short to generalize, however, given Republican control of the White House and Democratic control of Congress. While that situation changed in 1981, Congressional reassertion has continued. Thus, legislative assertiveness has been growing, and, while frequently overestimating Presidential power, we may not adequately recognize Congress's continuing role in domestic policy formation.

It is easy to see that the President cannot dominate Congress as he once could. While Edwards's (1980, 206) statement that "there is little the President can do about his degree of influence in Congress" may be too strong, a President today is inherently weaker in his dealings with Congress than Thomas Jefferson, or even Franklin Roosevelt or Lyndon Johnson. Therefore, as many other writers have observed, there is diminished potential for effective Presidential leadership.

WHAT CAN PRESIDENTS DO?

The President's power to achieve his goals is remarkably limited. Rarely is he able to accomplish policy outcomes for which he personally receives credit for their success. Presidents influence each policy actor but in turn are influenced by them to a greater degree than is commonly recognized. The formal resources available to the President in these interactions are counterbalanced by limitations on his power and also by the necessities of bargaining and persuasion (Neustadt 1980). Presidential impact is limited, then, because most policies require participation by other actors. Johnson could not alleviate poverty; Nixon could not secure approval for two of his Supreme Court nominees; Ford could not hold down federal spending; Carter could not get his preferred version of an energy program; and Reagan's aid to private schools seemed by early 1983 likely to go nowhere. In Presidential dealings with Congress, the trend since the first third of the twentieth century has usually been to usurp the functions of that body, most often with Congress's own acquiescence. But real or imagined Presidential abuses of the relationship have led recently to a Congressional rejuvenation.

A President's policy impact is typically indirect and limited because of his short tenure in office. The fact that policy gains are most often incremental suggests the limits on Presidential impact; it is a rare occurrence when Presidents are able to bring about large-scale changes in policy. In 1977 Carter and his close aides who occupied the White House found Presidential impact and policy change more elusive than they had anticipated. Thus, Presidential power to influence policy does not mean that control necessarily follows.

If the Carter Administration highlights the limitations of the Presidency, the Reagan Administration reveals its opportunities. James D. Barber (1980) was not the only one who was fooled into predicting that Reagan would be a passive President. It took Congress quite a while to realize that he had outfoxed them through the reconciliation process and other budget maneuvers that they themselves had written into law. But much of Reagan's real leadership in domestic policy was not legislative. He resurrected the "administrative Presidency" (Nathan 1983) through such techniques as executive orders, appointments to key positions, and administrative reorganizations. These techniques were revealed particularly in such policy areas as environmental affairs and civil rights (LeLoup and Shull 1982). What emerges most clearly in comparing Carter and Reagan is that the latter is a better politician. Carter was a moralist and Reagan an ideologue who was ultimately a pragmatist. Pragmatism usually wins out over moralism in politics. Still, Reagan's basically conservative ideology probably contributed to his weakened leadership beginning in 1982.

Virtually no systematic examination of Presidential impact in policymaking has been undertaken. Testing such impact requires an examination of Presidential influence and interactions in a number of stages and areas of policy. Presidents must excel on several conditions to exert policy influence: carefully selecting a small number of realistic legislative priorities; unusually skillful communications in order to build and sustain political coalitions around those priorities; ability to maintain a positive image and political popularity; adequate follow-through to ensure bureaucratic compliance and proper implementation; and finally, flexibility to modify policies in light of suggestions from carefully done policy evaluations. These conditions are reminiscent of policy stages, and, while we have made a start, there is considerable road to travel beyond policy formation, particularly toward implementation and evaluation.

ASSESSMENT

What can be concluded about actor roles in the policy formation process? Just because the policy process is dynamic does not mean that it can be altered easily or by large amounts. Policy tends to change slowly since government generally is conservative and frequently resists change. Policymakers will defer hard decisions if possible because political uncertainty encourages stability and continuity over change and innovation. Although policy change is normally a slow process in the United States, it is subject to adjustment by political leaders who can influence the process of domestic policy formation.

The overall formation (or development) of policy is complex. Frequently policies are modified through thorough evaluation or mere dissatisfaction with existing programs. Normally, however, policies are developed gradually (incrementally). Wildavsky asserts that such gradualism usually favors minor tinkering with old programs over creating entirely new ones (1979, 65). Sometimes no decision can also be a conscious policy action. Despite these characteristics of domestic policy formation, national elected officials appear to be rational and consistent. Policy intentions do seem to translate into policy actions.

Wildavsky spoke of two presidencies (domestic and foreign); Lowi's scheme suggests at least three; the substantive typology can envision six. How many are there? Probably the notion of a certain number is not as useful as it once was, but there is now markedly greater competition for influence in the domestic sphere, and both Congress and the President recognize the need for skillful accommodation. They may appear at times to be enemies, but partnership is the only road to success.

WHERE DO WE GO FROM HERE?

There are several things this book does and does not do. It provides a systematic analysis of the relationship of policy content and actor interaction within the policy formation process. Because it focuses on the early stages of public policy, it does not delve into implementation or evaluation of such policies. The research is truly comparative across six substantive areas of policy subsumed within three broader functional policy areas. The study can be replicated for other policy areas because explicit information is provided on measures.

The research departs from case analysis toward an examination of more aggregate behavior. This strategy facilitates comparison but does not allow for the richness frequently provided in detailed case analysis. Although some of the content of the policy areas is discussed, a comprehensive treatment of them is not possible here. The analysis, of necessity, is selective.

The study also has focused on interaction between Congress and the President. The exclusion of other actors does not diminish their recognized role in policy formation (for example, the bureaucracy in policy initiation). Besides Congress and the President, roles and influence for other governmental and nongovernmental actors can be posited (see Table 7-2). Any President finds other actor-groups asserting important roles in policy formation. The rest of the executive branch assists and may strongly influence the President in agenda-setting. He has a moderate amount of control over the executive branch and especially over the Presidential institutions (Executive Office of the President). The White House staff itself is a major source of policy ideas, and other organizations in the Executive Office (such as the domestic policy staff, National Security Council, and Council of Economic Advisers) and temporary

Table 7-2. Predicted Actor Influence

Policy Stage

Actor	Agenda – Setting	Formulation	Modification	Adoption
President	Moderately High	High	Moderately Low	Low
Congress	Moderately Low	Moderate	Moderately High	High
White House Staff	Moderately High	Moderately High	Low	Low
Bureaucracy	Moderate	Moderately High	Low	Low
Supreme Court	Low	Moderate	Moderately High	Moderate
Non govern- mental Groups	Moderately Low	Moderate	Moderate	Low

advisory bodies (including task forces, Presidential commissions, and White House conferences) may all play important roles in policy formation.

Recently there has been a heightened sensitivity to the fact that the bureaucracy makes, as well as carries out, policy decisions. (An interesting example is the controversy about health warnings on cigarette labels, where the FTC made rules and regulations virtually on its own in absence of Presidential and Congressional input; see Fritschler 1983.) Indeed, executive branch agencies may be one of the main sources of policy initiatives in the federal government.

The expected influence of the Supreme Court in policy formation may also be seen in Table 7-2. Even public opinion, interest groups, political parties, and the media may also be involved in policy formation, though not to the extent of their participation in policy advocacy or evaluation (see Shull 1979a). When public opinion has been shown to influence public policy, it generally has been post hoc—in monitoring and assessing rather than in agenda-setting or in initiating policy. Of these nongovernmental institutions, interest groups probably influence policy most in the earlier stages.

The predicted influences of all these entities in policy formation may be seen in Table 7-2. The influence of the White House staff parallels that of the President across the stages of policy formation. Lesser influence is attributed to nongovernmental groups, the Supreme Court, and the bureaucracy; their greatest role seems to be after the broad agenda is set, but before, during, and immediately after the formulation of Presidential initiatives to Congress.

This study has also been quite selective in the measurement of actor roles in policy formation. Executive orders and legislative liaison might be good indicators of policy initiation, but they are not dealt with here. I have had to be selective. Other possible measures are discussed in the Appendix, but many conceptual and measurement problems exist with them as well. Other indicators and policy areas should be explored in recognition that there are limitations to what can be established through the analysis of aggregate data.

Widely differing roles and responsibilities have been shown to exist, even within what is frequently perceived as a single (beginning) stage of public policy. But policy formation is much more complex than commonly assumed, and this preliminary effort has just scratched the surface of that complexity. Not only do we need clearer conceptualization of the meaning of policy terms, but better measures are required to tap the numerous components of policy formation and subsequent stages in the policy process. Nevertheless, this report of aggregate data has accomplished its limited goal of examining changes in actor roles across areas and stages of policy formation.

NOTES

1. Light (1982, 133) believes that Ford would have been a more assertive President had he served longer.

2. Truman is almost impossible to compare, however, due to the lack of equivalent data.

Methodological
Appendix

The discussion of coding, indicators, levels of generality, and methods used in this study was kept rather brief throughout the text for three reasons. First, an introductory statement on sources of data and indicators was provided in Chapter 1. Second, subsequent chapters explored further into the nature of alternative indicators for Presidential-Congressional interaction at each policy substage. Finally, this Methodological Appendix is provided for those desiring more detail on data, measurement, and coding procedures, particularly with respect to how issues fit into the typologies and problems with the indicators used.

This study has tried to discern four relatively distinct steps in policy formation: agenda-setting (through Presidential statements), initiation (Presidential actions to propose legislation), modification (Congressional change in and/or support for Presidential positions), and adoption (the legislative success of Presidential proposals). The study considered the degree of consistency that exists (for example, whether statements by the President translate into legislative actions). Aggregate data cannot establish these relationships with certainty but can suggest whether there are fruitful avenues for further inquiry. Broad substantive categories were purposely selected because if they have discriminating value, then the worth of these categorizations (particularly the narrower ones included) should be established. After discussing the time frame for this study, this Appendix devotes considerable attention to coding procedures for both the functional and substantive policy areas. A section on analysis and conceptual problems with the incorporated measures concludes this Appendix.

LEVELS OF GENERALITY

The data for this research were collected from a variety of primary and secondary sources for 1953 through 1975. Some data are available from 1945 or through 1982. The research was conducted on several different levels, summarized below, ranging from the most to the least aggregated:

1. Comparisons of policy areas across all Presidential Administrations are made to see where statements and actions are greatest and least.
2. Comparisons between the two political parties are made. The Republican years (1953-60, 1969-76, 1981-) differ in emphasis from Democratic Administrations (1945-52, 1961-68, 1977-80).
3. Individual Administrations are compared to see if the thrust of policymaking has altered over time, both within one Administration and among all Presidential terms.
4. Finally, yearly comparisons are possible. Although fewer data points are available, such an analysis leaves the data in their purest, least aggregated form. Perhaps less amenable to generalization, the direct translation of specific statements into specific policy actions can best be observed on a yearly basis. Of particular interest are first, last, and reelection years within each Administration. Such groupings can then be reaggregated, thereby capturing more data points.

Data are also examined overall, then by functional policy area, and then by the various levels of substantive disaggregation, frequently to the case level. These substantive levels may be reviewed in Chapter 1, Table 1-1.

CODING PROCEDURES

Functional Areas

Congressional Quarterly's (CQ) box score of yearly Presidential proposals to Congress and approval thereof is used to measure policy initiation and adoption. These data are available in comparable form only from 1953 through 1975. The data points for the three functional areas (distributive, regulatory, and redistributive) may be seen in Figure A-1. Over 5,700 Presidential initiatives to Congress were identified by CQ for these years, but the difficulties of classifying into the Lowi typology went beyond the mere number of cases. Although Lowi gives some examples in his various works, he provides "little guidance for determining how a policy is to be classified in any but the simplest cases" (Greenberg et al. 1977, 1534). Not only do some substantive issues fall within more than one category, but issues may also change their designation over time (Wilson 1973, 329; Kessel 1977, 434; Greenberg et al. 1977; Vogler 1977, 264).

Overlap among the substantive issues within Lowi's three policy types did occur. Several examples illustrate the problems and the gray areas. Health policy can be all three (distributive if one is referring to subsidies or construction; regulatory if the concern is smoking, pollution, or radiation control; and redistributive when the issue is national health insurance or Medicaid). Welfare policy is normally classified as redistributive, but some instances of each of the other two categories were found. A third example is agriculture, where Lowi himself admits considerable overlap across categories (1970, 325). Some agricultural issues, such as the Food for Peace Plan or food stamps, were clearly redistributive and were so labeled.

A study by the author categorized all Presidential initiatives to Congress according to the Lowi typology (Shull 1983b). Data were classified routinely into the substantive issues that have been identified by various authors as fitting Lowi's scheme. In most cases, that procedure allowed subcategories of those initiatives (as designated by CQ in its box score) to be left intact. An element of judgment, if not sheer intuition, comes into play, however, when coding initiatives that deviate from CQ designations. (The substantive issues decided upon in each category appear in Table A-1.) Since 22 percent of the initiatives were not classified (civil defense, executive reorganization, and the District of Columbia, among others), either because of clear overlap or ambiguity, the categories are believed to be relatively pure. By accepting CQ rules, except for stated exceptions and the residual category, the classification seems replicable.

Both pre- and post-hoc coding rules were devised. Despite prior acceptance of most CQ categories, coding of specific initiatives

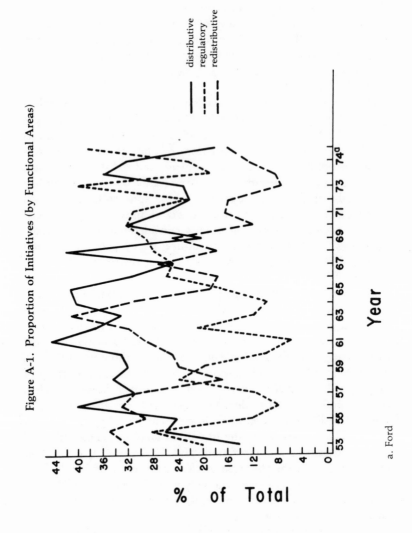

Figure A-1. Proportion of Initiatives (by Functional Areas)

a. Ford

186

Table A-1. Substantive Issues Classified by the Lowi Typology

Distributive	Regulatory	Redistributive	Not Classified
Grants, loans, contracts, construction (health, education, space, military)	Natural resources (land use, strip mining, environment, energy controls)	Welfare, poverty, almost all civil rights (voting, public accommodations, busing, desegregation, age, sex, race)	National security and space (when not research and development)
Public works (water projects, parks, recreation)	Regulation of communication, transportation, atomic power, food and drug	American Indians	Civil defense
Agriculture (most issues including subsidies)			Treaties
		Unemployment, minimum wage, labor benefits	Military assistance
Soil conservation	Trade (imports and exports, customs)	Public housing, rent control	Territories and statehood
Research and development (space, atomic, transportation, all training programs)	Most economic issues (anti-trust, oil price controls)	Social Security	Reorganization, create new agencies
		Medicare, Medicaid	Civil service (pay raises, awards, federal employment)
Federalism issues	Labor restrictions	Taxation (especially changes in burdens)	Selective Service, draft
Area redevelopment	Crime and internal security	Foreign economic aid	Presidential disability
Impacted aid	Consumer protection	Immigration (quotas, refugees)	District of Columbia
Government services	Election reform	Famine relief	General government
Post Office	Pollution, smoking laws, radiation control	Foodstamps, Food for Peace	
Veterans benefits	General rules, controls, reforms	Urban renewal	
Revenue sharing			

Note: Defining characteristics identified by Lowi and others were also considered in classifying initiatives.

187

frequently required later judgments. A list of analytical characteristics identified by Lowi and others (mentioned in Chapter 1) was
also used in the coding operation, particularly for those initiatives
not automatically fitting one of the Lowi categories. Other defining
features for each policy type, such as the amount of competition,
the locus of decision making, the breadth of policy impact, whether
benefits are zero-sum, and the degree of logrolling were helpful in
the classification when the content of the measure alone was an
insufficient guide to placement. But there is surprising agreement
among authors about the fit of most substantive issues to the
functional typology (Ripley and Franklin 1980; Hayes 1978; Lowi
1972).

All coding was done by the author, but as a reliability check, a
graduate student independently coded initiatives for two randomly
selected years. Because the coding was into discrete categories, not
on a continuum, a percentage score is more appropriate than correlation as a measure of coder reliability (Gurr 1972, 58). Although
there are no particular guidelines for agreement, the resulting score
was 91 percent. The residual (nonclassified) category no doubt kept
agreement high, and reliability probably would have been reduced
below tolerable limits without the residual category (values deleted
in Figure A-1) or if Lowi's constituent category had been included.
It should be noted that rather high success in classifying component
substantive issues may give some credence to the analytically
muddled functional typology but does not guarantee that it contains an underlying theoretical dimension.

Substantive Areas

The data varied in availability and completeness across the four
stages of policy formation. The two substantive areas used in each
of the three Lowi categories appear to reflect distributive, regulatory, and redistributive categories rather well. The index of
Public Papers of the Presidents of the United States was relied on
heavily for coding the data on Presidential agenda-setting. This
index provides the most comprehensive key words listing, defining
each substantive area seen in Table A-2. These key words and the
categorizations provided by CQ are used to fit narrower subissues
into broader substantive areas, and those to the functional areas.

This procedure is easier, more self-explanatory, and more generally accepted. The key words presented in Table A-2 incorporate those both included and excluded from the analysis.

The measures of Presidential preferences in agenda-setting ultimately incorporated were discussed in Chapter 2. Before accepting items (title of each document) and policy statements (Presidential focus on particular issue), several other potential indicators were initially considered.

Sending messages to Congress provides a means of focusing legislative, media, and public attention on the President's program. Such communications also provide a measure of the level of Presidential activity with Congress. Today, there are several formal messages each year, including State of the Union, Budget, and Economic Report. Some messages, such as the State of the Union, are in broad policy strokes and, in recent years, have been delivered by the President in person before a joint session of Congress. Truman was the first President to deliver such annual messages personally to Congress. Carter was an exception to this norm, sending rather than personally delivering his outgoing 1981 address. Any number of special messages, letters, reports, and other documents may also be sent to Congress. The average number of messages, with the exception of Eisenhower, increased in each successive Administration, perhaps due in part to advances in communications technology. The average number of letters, however, has varied (see Table A-3).

Agenda-setting is probably better tapped through overall items and statements than by looking only at the President's communications to Congress. The latter often are letters or other messages seeking Congressional action rather than stating broader policy preferences. A comparison of items and communications is provided in Figure A-2. The relationship between these two variables is moderate ($r = .41$), not surprising since the latter is a subset of the former.

Items and communications have been presented here in the aggregate; they have not been distinguished by importance. Some are major speeches, such as the State of the Union Address, while others are relatively insignificant letters or routine pronouncements. Such a weighting, or at least a differentiation in type of item or communication (for example, major speech, special message,

Table A-2. Key Words for Categorizing Substantive Issues

Distributive

Price Supports	Excludes	Public Works	Excludes
agricultural surplus/quota commodities (as general heading & specific crops) acreage allotments, diversion programs excess land, parity production controls National Food Bank	school lunch foreign agri. disaster relief conservation loans soil bank tariffs rural development	flood control/dams/water projects irrigation/conservation public lands/parks/wildlife refuges transportation/highways/mass transit/aid to airports/rail travel navigation/saline conversion oceanography, rivers & harbors power, communications, ports	drought sewerage/waste oil exploration atomic/nuclear energy solar heating outer continetal shelf construction
Agencies: Commodity Credit Corporation (CCC).		**Agencies:** Army Corps of Engineers, Bureau of Reclamation, St. Lawrence Seaway.	

Regulatory

Crime	Excludes	Anti-Trust	Excludes
enforcement, police specific types crime	rights of accused	mergers, monopoly, deregulation of business	business subsidies

190

small business
loans

crimes by public
officials
contempt of Con-
gress
corruption

atomic security, skyjacking
juvenile delinquency

(organized, drug, riot)
internal security,
espionage
penalties, victim compensation

Clayton Act
Sherman Act
laissez-faire
holding company

Agencies: FBI, Law Enforcement Assistance
Administration.

Agencies: Federal Trade Commission,
Securities and Exchange Commission.

Redistributive

Civil Rights

	Excludes
discrimination/equal opportunity/rights, quotas (voting, age, race, sex) public accommodations	broader issues like rights of accused, censorship, Bill of Rights
White House Conference on Public Schools (desegregation, integration, busing, local option, vouchers)	

Agencies: Justice Department,
Civil Rights Division, HEW
Office for Civil Rights.

Poverty

	Excludes
welfare/poor/economically disadvantaged/dependency	issues not specifically for poor, such as: Medicare, Social Security, veterans bene- fits, handi- capped, day care, higher education (except BEOG)
employment (opportunities, minimum wage, compensation, job creation)	
housing (subsidized, public only)	
Medicaid, Food Stamps, ESEA, CETA, AFDC, Head Start, rat control	
migrant workers, depressed areas	

Agencies: Departments of HEW
and HUD, Office of Economic
Opportunity.

Note: Reflects level III generality from Table 1-1.

Table A-3. Presidential Communications

President	Year In Office	Messages to/about Congress Number	Messages to/about Congress Ave. # per yr.	Letters to/about Congress Number	Letters to/about Congress Ave. # per yr.	Total Communications Number	Total Communications Ave. # per yr.
Roosevelt	12	--	--	--	--	--	--
Truman	8	244	31	118	15	362	45
Eisenhower	8	157	20	62	8	219	27
Kennedy	3	63	21	97	32	160	53
Johnson	5	242	48	100	20	342	68
Nixon	5.5	356	65	50	9	406	74
Ford (1976 missing)	1.5	121	81	59	39	180	120
Carter (1977)	1	103	103	117	117	220	220

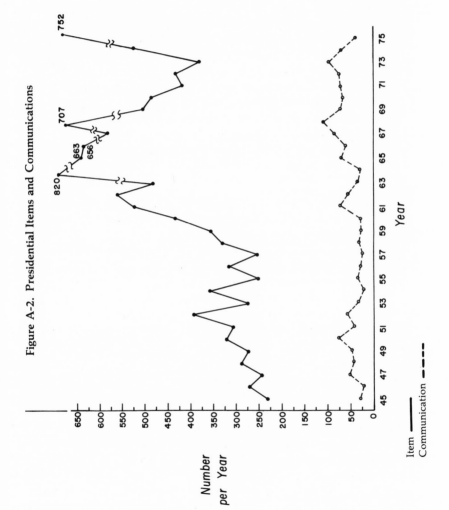

Figure A-2. Presidential Items and Communications

193

letter, other communication), would probably be desirable in further utilization of these measures. Communications, like statements, could be content-analyzed to ascertain specific Presidential agendas, but the aggregate presentation here is simply to suggest different measures of such rhetoric.

Finally, as an indicator of importance of particular statements, the number of printed lines within each policy statement was considered. Although number of lines is potentially useful as a measure of salience of an issue, variety of print and column size used in the *Public Papers* limits the utility of the measure. While approximate parity (number of words per line) is achieved by multiplying lines in certain years (1953-60, 1974-76) by a factor of 1.8, the measure was subsequently dropped from the analysis.

The policy statement is the unit of analysis for determining Presidential agenda preferences. Examples of policy statements by Ford (1976) on price supports follow:

1. The President "concurred with the actions of the Secretary of Agriculture to raise dairy price supports to 80 percent after April 1": supportive, eight lines.

2. Veto of milk price supports bill, urging "Congress to join him in his effort to hold down federal spending, milk surpluses, and consumer prices": nonsupportive, forty-two lines.

3. Although he is going to recommend expansion of farm programs for several years, he wants to "encourage farmers to produce for the open market with no surplus": mixed or neutral, eighteen lines.

Obvious problems with these measures of Presidential agenda-setting will be evident to even the casual observer. The Presidential agenda as here determined is limited strictly to public utterances of the President. A way to measure informal communications has not yet been found. Thus, it is not claimed that the full extent of Presidential preferences has been measured. However, since items and statements can come from the whole span of Presidential documents (even letters and press conferences), we have at least tapped a wider range of potential agenda preferences than studies limited strictly to the State of the Union Address.

MEASUREMENT

Analysis Techniques

Problems of data generation frequently are magnified in their subsequent analysis. Some of the data incorporated here have been analyzed successfully in other contexts. Thousands of Presidential initiatives were made to Congress during the years analyzed. Nevertheless, controlling simultaneously for specific policy areas and subareas, Administrations, actor roles, or other narrower concerns greatly diminishes the number of cases available for sophisticated empirical testing. Descriptive statistics and bivariate measures of association are adopted as the most appropriate tools for testing these expectations. Thus, means, percentages, and simple correlation (r) appear most frequently. Occasionally, multiple regression is used to control for the effects of time. Significance tests (Cramer's V) are used where a sample rather than a population of data is available.

Indicators: Problems and Promise

Because agenda-setting was discussed earlier, we can limit the present discussion to measures of the subsequent stages of policy formation. The four measures discussed here were all compiled by CQ. The CQ measure of Presidential initiatives and subsequent legislative approval (adoption) provides numerous advantages to scholars. This box score is a tangible indicator of Presidential preferences and is compiled from *Weekly Compilation of Presidential Documents.* Not only can we examine these initiatives in any given year and across time, but we can also compare individual Presidents and policy areas. CQ categorizes them into major policy areas (such as Public Works and Resources) and also into subissues (such as water). The box score is one of the few nonbudgetary measures of Presidential preferences and indicates which issues are salient to Presidents. The indicators of initiatives and success are also reflective of the health of the President's legislative relations. Because of these decided benefits, a number of other studies have used this box score measure to examine the process of policymaking (Wayne 1978; Edwards 1980; Ripley 1979), while others have looked at differences in the content of these proposals (Wildavsky 1966; LeLoup and Shull, 1979a).

Unfortunately, the disadvantages of the data are just as pronounced, leading CQ to abandon the box score measure after 1975. Since there is no public record of which bills introduced in Congress originate from the Administration, the measure may or may not reflect actual legislative proposals. It is unclear what source CQ used prior to the publication of the *Weekly Compilation* in 1965, but in a letter to the author, Research Director Robert Cuthrell presumed that *Public Papers* and other documents were sources for initiatives. Nevertheless, it was a CQ judgment about whether an issue mentioned in a Presidential statement constituted an actual legislative request. If more than one Presidential remark was directed toward the issue, only the most definitive statement was used to track through the legislative process. Congressional Quarterly then made a judgment as to whether subsequent legislation amounted to acceptance or rejection of a President's initial request.

Another objection to the success measure is that it is insensitive to the time clock of Congress (Cohen 1980, 4). Thus, an initiative not passed in one year counts against the President, even if it passes in the second year of the legislative biennium. Unfortunately, the box score data are aggregated; there is no score for individual legislators or even knowledge that a recorded vote was taken on the initiative. Additionally, the box score is alleged to measure only one type of success: public (floor) action. Another criticism is that all requests are weighted equally, and thus trivial issues are not distinguished from major ones. This latter charge is not totally accurate since most major requests appear in the form of multiple initiatives (Shull 1981; Shull and LeLoup 1981, 564).

An initiative may never become a bill, and it is a bit like adding apples and oranges to measure legislative approval of something Congress may never even have considered. Yet more direct measures have proven elusive. Even if it were available, a list from the White House or the Office of Management and the Budget (OMB) of all bills introduced on behalf of the Administration might be unreliable. Indeed, White House lists frequently show higher success rates because of the temptation to omit bills from the list not approved by Congress. For example, White House liaison chief Lawrence O'Brien's list for 1965 shows a 90 percent success rate

(*Congressional Quarterly Almanac*, 1965, 112). Despite problems of equivalence across Administrations, Light's (1982) utilization of proposals "in accordance with" the President's programs, as determined by OMB, is a promising source of data.

Observers are also aware that despite central program clearance, not all Administration bills are Presidential priorities. CQ's principal apprehension about its own box score seems to be that writers were quoting aggregate figures (of Presidential success, for example) without adequately considering the substance of the initiatives themselves or qualitative or other quantitative factors that may influence the results. This criticism seems valid, as the measure does not reveal the relative ranking of proposals by the President. Although CQ does not weigh initiatives by importance, we have mentioned that major initiatives frequently have several parts and thus count for more than one initiative (*Congressional Quarterly Almanac*, 1963, 86). The question of how initiatives are changed by Congress also persists. High success may merely reveal what Congress also wants or that a President has initiated relatively few proposals in the first place.

Finally, CQ is itself to blame in large part for encouraging misuse of the data. In virtually every one of the box score reports, the same kind of aggregate figures were used that it cringes at seeing in other sources. ("Congress Grants 47.6 percent of Johnson's Specific Requests," *Congressional Quarterly Almanac*, 1967, 161.) Despite problems with the box score, CQ was providing a valuable service for scholars and journalists alike. It is discriminating across substantive policy areas and the measure seems no less reliable than CQ's indicator of support (legislative approval of the President's position on roll call votes before Congress). With this support measure, similar content analysis judgments of Presidential positions are required. At least as much margin for error exists in the support indicator, and occasionally Administration spokesmen will be the source of the President's position. At least with the initiatives measure, the request comes directly from the President, since it must appear in one of his public statements.

The support measure was our primary indicator of Congressional modification. Beyond mere support by Congress for Presidents' positions, I looked at several related aspects: the likelihood of Presidents to take positions, whether such votes were more or less frequently amendments, the partisan voting that occurs (for example, party vote if 50 percent of one party votes against 50 percent of the other), and the voting conflict that occurs on these roll calls. The formula for this latter measure of conflict is as follows:

$$1 - \frac{\left| \dfrac{\text{Yea}_1\text{-Nay}_1 \ldots + \text{Yea}_n\text{-Nay}_n}{\text{total}_1 \qquad\qquad \text{total}_n} \right|}{\text{TOTAL}}.$$

Some assert that support is a better measure of Presidential relations with Congress than is success (Sigelman 1979; Zeidenstein 1981). Indeed, it is argued that the key votes subset of the support measure eliminates the problem of triviality. Problems also exist with the support indicator, however, and one is often quite unsure of what is being measured (Shull and LeLoup 1981; Shull 1981). At least with the measure of success, CQ has made a conscientious attempt to guarantee that the final approved bill was in accord with the initial request (Edwards 1980, 13-18). Thus, we simply compare success and support (as was done in Chapter 5). Both measures have advantages and disadvantages and appear to differ from each other both conceptually and empirically.

CQ provides documentation on how the support measure was collected (see *Congressional Quarterly Weekly Reports*, 12/9/78, 3409). It could expand upon the terse presentation for success, and the coding rules could be made just as reliable. CQ ground rules for the box score are not very explicit. About all we are told is that the request must be specific, not merely an endorsement or call for legislative study. Also excluded are nominations and most annual appropriations. (For an example of the rules, see *Congressional Quarterly Almanac*, 1974, 943.) The organization could devise schemes to weigh the initiatives by importance and also provide other indicators for comparison, such as the President's partisan margin in Congress.

It should be obvious that some of the incorporated measures are crude and tentative. Probably none of them provides perfect pictures of reality. Considerable problems also are associated with utilizing these quantitative measures across time. It is probable that they are influenced by a multiplicity of factors, only some of which were covered in this research. But the way to improve measurement is not to ignore it. CQ should begin collecting initiatives to Congress again. Only by having such data available can we and they work toward improvement.

It should also be heartening to readers of this book that there are more data possibilities in these largely unexplored areas of research than have commonly been recognized. A wide array of indicators of actor roles and behavior has been presented, which should help discern the degree of rationality that exists in policy formation. The extent to which statements by the President and actions by both Congress and the President are interpretable demonstrates the complexity of the policy formation process, but it also offers testimony to the utility of using actor roles and policy content to help explain these complex phenomena.

References

Allison, Graham T. 1971. *Essence of Decision: Explaining the Cuban Missile Crisis.* Boston: Little, Brown.

Anderson, James E. (ed.). 1982. *Cases in Public Policy-Making.* 2d ed. New York: Holt, Rinehart and Winston.

_____. 1979. *Public Policy-Making.* 2d ed. New York: Holt, Rinehart and Winston.

_____; David W. Brady; and Charles S. Bullock III. 1978. *Public Policy and Politics in America.* North Scituate, Mass.: Duxbury Press.

Andrews, Wayne (ed.). 1958. *Autobiography of Theodore Roosevelt.* New York: Charles Scribner's Sons.

Barber, James D. 1980. "Worrying about Reagan." *New York Times,* September 8: 19.

Bauer, Raymond; Ithiel Pool; and Lewis Dexter. 1972. *American Business and Public Policy.* Rev. ed. Chicago: Aldine-Atherton.

Berkowitz, Edward D. 1980. "Politics of Mental Retardation during the Kennedy Administration." *Social Science Quarterly* 61 (June): 128-43.

Broder, David S. 1982. "Reagan's Equivocal Year." *New Orleans Times-Picayune,* January 21: 11.

Burns, James M. 1965. *Presidential Government.* Boston: Houghton Mifflin.

Chamberlain, Lawrence H. 1946. "President, Congress and Legislation." *Political Science Quarterly* 61 (March): 42-60.

Chandler, Marsha; William Chandler; and David Vogler. 1974. "Policy Analysis and the Search for Theory." *American Politics Quarterly* 2 (January): 107-18.

Chelf, Carl P. 1981. *Public Policymaking in America.* Santa Monica: Goodyear Publishing Co.

Clausen, Aage R. 1973. *How Congressmen Decide: A Policy Focus.* New York: St. Martin's Press.

Cobb, Roger W., and Charles P. Elder. 1972. *Participation in American Politics: Dynamics of Agenda-Building.* Baltimore: Johns Hopkins University Press.

Cohen, Jeffery E. 1980. "Impact of the Modern Presidency on Presidential Programmatic Success." Presented at the American Political Science Association Convention, Washington, D.C., August 28-31.

Congressional Quarterly Almanac (annual). Washington, D.C.: Congressional Quarterly.

Congressional Quarterly Weekly Reports. Washington, D.C.: Congressional Quarterly.

Cronin, Thomas E. 1980. *State of the Presidency.* 2d ed. Boston: Little, Brown.

Davis, Eric. 1979. "Legislative Liaison in the Carter Administration." *Political Science Quarterly* 95 (Summer): 287-301.

Dodd, Lawrence C. 1977. "Congress and the Quest for Power." In Lawrence C. Dodd and Bruce I. Oppenheimer, eds., *Congress Reconsidered,* 269-307. New York: Praeger Publishers.

Donovan, John C. 1974. *The Cold Warriors: A Policy-Making Elite.* Lexington, Mass.: D. C. Heath and Co.

_____. 1973. *Politics of Poverty.* 2d ed. Indianapolis: Pegasus.

_____. 1970. *Policy Makers.* New York: Western Publishing Co.

Edelman, Murray. 1974. "The Politics of Persuasion." In James D. Barber, ed., *Choosing the President,* 149-74. Englewood Cliffs, N.J.: Prentice-Hall.

Edwards, George C. III. 1980. *Presidential Influence in Congress.* San Francisco: W. H. Freeman.

_____. 1978. "Presidential Electoral Performance as a Source of Presidential Power." *American Journal of Political Science* 22 (February): 152-68.

_____, and Ira Sharkansky. 1978. *Policy Predicament.* San Francisco: W. H. Freeman and Co.

Eyestone, Robert. 1978. *From Social Issues to Public Policy.* New York: John Wiley and Sons.

Fairlie, Henry. 1973. *The Kennedy Promise: Politics of Expectation.* New York: Dell Publishing Co.

Ferejohn, John. 1974. *Porkbarrel Politics.* Palo Alto: Stanford University Press.

Fiorina, Morris P., and Roger G. Noll. 1979. "Majority Rule Models and Legislative Elections." *Journal of Politics* 41 (November): 1081-1104.

Fritschler, A. Lee. 1983. *Smoking and Politics: Policymaking and the Federal Bureaucracy.* 3d ed. Englewood Cliffs: Prentice-Hall.

Froman, Lewis A. 1968. "The Categorization of Policy Contents." In Austin Ranney, ed., *Political Science and Public Policy,* 41-54. Chicago: Markham Publishing Co.

Fry, Brian R., and Richard F. Winters. 1970. "Politics of Redistribution." *American Political Science Review* 64 (June): 508-22.

Gallagher, Hugh G. 1977. "The President, Congress and Legislation." In Thomas Cronin and Rexford Tugwell, eds., *The Presidency Reappraised*, 2d ed., 267-82. New York: Praeger Publishers.

———. 1974. "Presidents, Congress, and the Legislative Functions." In Rexford Tugwell and Thomas Cronin, eds., *The Presidency Reappraised*, 217-33. New York: Praeger Publishers.

Greenberg, George D.; Jeffrey A. Miller; Lawrence B. Mohr; and Bruce C. Vladeck. 1977. "Developing Public Policy Theory: Perspectives from Empirical Research." *American Political Science Review* 71 (December): 1532-43.

Gurr, Ted R. 1972. *Polimetrics*. Englewood Cliffs, N.J.: Prentice-Hall.

Hammond, Thomas H., and Jane M. Fraser. 1980. "Faction Size, the Conservative Coalition, and the Determinants of Presidential 'Success' in Congress." Presented at the American Political Science Association Convention, Washington, D.C., August 28-30.

Hargrove, Erwin C. 1974. *Power of the Modern Presidency*. New York: Alfred A. Knopf, Inc.

Hayes, Michael T. 1978. "Semi-Sovereign Pressure Groups: A Critique of Current Theory and an Alternative Typology." *Journal of Politics* 40 (February): 134-61.

Hofferbert, Richard I. 1974. *Study of Public Policy*. Indianapolis: Bobbs-Merrill.

Huntington, Samuel P. 1961. *Common Defense: Strategic Problems in National Politics*. New York: Columbia University Press.

Jacob, Charles E. 1977. "The Congressional Elections and Outlook." In Gerald Pomper, ed., *The Election of 1976: Reports and Interpretations*, 83-105. New York: David McKay Co.

James, Dorothy B. 1973. *Contemporary Presidency*. 2d ed. New York: Pegasus.

Johannes, John R. 1972a. *Policy Innovation in Congress*. Morristown, N.J.: General Learning Press.

———. 1972b. "Where Does the Buck Stop? Congress, President, and the Responsibility for Legislative Initiation." *Western Political Quarterly* 25 (September): 396-415.

Jones, Charles O. 1977. *Introduction to the Study of Public Policy*. 2d ed. North Scituate, Mass.: Duxbury Press.

Katzmann, Robert H. 1981. *Regulatory Policy: The Federal Trade Commission and Antitrust Policy.* Cambridge: MIT Press.

Kearns, Doris. 1976. *Lyndon Johnson and the American Dream.* New York: Harper and Row.

Kessel, John H. 1977. "Seasons of Presidential Politics." *Social Science Quarterly* 58 (December): 418-35.

_____. 1975. *Domestic Presidency.* North Scituate, Mass.: Duxbury Press.

_____. 1974. "Parameters of Presidential Politics." *Social Science Quarterly* 55 (June): 8-24.

Kingdon, John W. 1981. *Congressmen's Voting Decisions.* 2d ed. New York: Harper and Row.

LeLoup, Lance T. 1975. "Agency Policy Actions: Determinants of Nonincremental Change." In Randall B. Ripley and Grace A. Franklin, eds., *Policy-Making in the Federal Executive Branch,* 65-90. New York: Free Press.

_____, and Steven A. Shull. 1982. "Presidential Policy Making in Civil Rights." Presented at the American Political Science Association Convention, Denver, September 2-5.

_____. 1979a. "Congress vs. the Executive: The 'Two Presidencies' Reconsidered." *Social Science Quarterly* 59 (March): 704-19.

_____. 1979b. "Dimensions of Presidential Policy Making." In Steven A. Shull and Lance T. LeLoup, eds., *The Presidency: Studies in Public Policy,* 3-19. Brunswick, Ohio: King's Court Communications.

Light, Paul C. 1982. *The President's Agenda: Domestic Policy Choice from Kennedy to Carter.* Baltimore: Johns Hopkins University Press.

Lindblom, Charles. 1980. *The Policy-Making Process.* 2d ed. Englewood Cliffs, N.J.: Prentice-Hall.

Lowi, Theodore J. 1972. "Four Systems of Policy, Politics, and Choice." *Public Administration Review* 32 (July-August): 298-310.

_____. 1970. "Decision-Making v. Policy Making: Toward an Antidote for Technocracy." *Public Administration Review* 30 (May-June): 314-25.

_____. 1964. "American Business, Public Policy, Case Studies, and Political Theory." *World Politics* 16 (July): 677-715.

Maass, Arthur. 1951. *Muddy Waters.* Cambridge: Harvard University Press.

McConnell, Grant. 1976. *The Modern Presidency.* 2d ed. New York: St. Martin's Press.

_____. 1963. *Steel and the Presidency—1962.* New York: W. W. Norton and Company.

MacRae, Duncan, and James Wilde. 1979. *Policy Analysis for Public Decisions.* North Scituate, Mass.: Duxbury Press.

Mayhew, David R. 1966. *Party Loyalty among Congressmen.* Cambridge: Harvard University Press.

Moe, Ronald C., and Steven C. Teel. 1970. "Congress as Policy Maker: A Necessary Reappraisal." *Political Science Quarterly* 85 (September): 443-70.

Morgan, Ruth P. 1970. *The President and Civil Rights.* New York: St. Martin's Press.

Mueller, John E. 1973. *War, Presidents and Public Opinion.* New York: John Wiley and Sons.

Nathan, Richard P. 1983. *The Administrative Presidency.* 2d ed. New York: John Wiley and Sons.

National Journal (selected issues). Washington, D.C.: Government Research Corporation.

Neustadt, Richard E. 1980. *Presidential Power.* New York: John Wiley and Sons.

_____. 1973. "Politicians and Bureaucrats." In David Truman, ed., *The Congress and America's Future,* 2d ed., 118-40. Englewood Cliffs: Prentice-Hall.

_____. 1955. "Presidency and Legislation: Planning the President's Program." *American Political Science Review* 49 (December): 980-1021.

Orfield, Gary. 1975. *Congressional Power: Congress and Social Change.* New York: Harcourt Brace Jovanovich.

Ostrom, Elinor. 1980. "Is It B or Not-B? That Is the Question." *Social Science Quarterly* 61 (September): 198-202.

Peppers, Donald A. 1975. "Two Presidencies: Eight Years Later." In Aaron Wildavsky, ed., *Perspectives on the Presidency,* 462-71. Boston: Little, Brown.

Polsby, Nelson W. 1976. *Congress and the Presidency.* 3d ed. Englewood Cliffs: Prentice-Hall.

_____. 1969. "Policy Analysis and Congress." *Public Policy* 18 (Fall): 61-74.

Pomper, Gerald M. 1980. *Elections in America.* 2d ed. New York: Longman.

Public Papers of the Presidents of the United States (yearly). Washington, D.C.: Government Printing Office.

Ranney, Austin (ed.). 1968. *Political Science and Public Policy.* Chicago: Markham Publishing Co.

Redford, Emmett S. 1969. *Democracy in the Administrative State.* New York: Oxford University Press.

Ripley, Randall B. 1979. "Carter and Congress." In Steven A. Shull and Lance T. LeLoup, eds., *The Presidency: Studies in Public Policy,* 65-82. Brunswick, Ohio: King's Court Communications.

_____. 1972. *Kennedy and Congress.* Morristown, N.J.: General Learning Press.

_____, and Grace A. Franklin. 1982. *The Bureaucracy and Policy Implementation.* Homewood, Ill.: Dorsey Press.

_____. 1980. *Congress, the Bureaucracy and Public Policy.* 2d ed. Homewood, Ill.: Dorsey Press.

_____ (eds.). 1975. *Policy Making in the Federal Executive Branch.* New York: Free Press.

Robinson, James A. 1967. *Congress and Foreign Policy-Making: A Study in Legislative Influence and Initiative.* Rev. ed. Homewood, Ill.: Dorsey Press.

Rodgers, Harrel R., and Charles S. Bullock III. 1972. *Law and Social Change.* New York: McGraw-Hill.

Salisbury, Robert, and John Heinz. 1970. "A Theory of Policy Analysis and Some Preliminary Applications." In Ira Sharkansky, ed., *Policy Analysis in Political Science,* 39-60. Chicago: Markham Publishing Co.

Schwarz, John E., and L. Earl Shaw. 1976. *U.S. Congress in Comparative Perspective.* Hinsdale, Ill.: Dryden Press.

Shank, Alan. 1980. *Presidential Policy Leadership: Kennedy and Social Welfare.* Lanham, Md.: University Press of America.

Sharkansky, Ira. 1970. *Routines of Politics.* New York: D. Van Nostrand-Reinholt.

Shinn, Don C. 1980. "Towards a Model for Presidential Influence in Congress." Presented at the American Political Science Association Convention, Washington, D.C., August 28-31.

Shull, Steven A. 1983a. "Identifying Presidents' Domestic Agendas." *Social Science Quarterly* 64 (March) 163-72.

_____. 1983b. "Change in Presidential Policy Initiatives." *Western Political Quarterly* 36 (September): forthcoming.

_____. 1981. "Assessing Measures of Presidential-Congressional Policy Making." *Presidential Studies Quarterly* 11 (Spring): 151-57.

_____. 1979a. *Presidential Policy Making: An Analysis.* Brunswick, Ohio: King's Court Communications.

_____. 1979b. "An Agency's Best Friend: The White House or Congress?" In Steven A. Shull and Lance T. LeLoup, eds., *The Presidency: Studies in Public Policy,* 219-38. Brunswick, Ohio: King's Court Communications.

_____. 1978. "Presidential-Congressional Support for Agencies and for Each Other: A Comparative Look." *Journal of Politics* 40 (August): 453-60.

_____, and Lance T. LeLoup. 1981. "Reassessing the Reassessment: Comment on Sigelman's Note on the 'Two Presidencies' Thesis." *Journal of Politics* 43 (May): 563-64.

_____, and Edward V. Heck. 1980. "Justices and Presidents: Issue Salience and Policy Agreement." Presented at the American Political Science Association Convention, Washington, D.C., August 28-31.

Sigelman, Lee. 1979. "Reassessing the 'Two Presidencies' Thesis." *Journal of Politics* 41 (November): 1195-1205.

Spitzer, Robert J. 1980. "President as Policy Maker: Arenas of Presidential Power from 1954-1974." Presented at the American Political Science Association Convention, Washington, D.C., August 28-31.

_____. 1979. "The Presidency and Public Policy: A Preliminary Inquiry." *Presidential Studies Quarterly* 9 (Fall): 441-57.

Steinberger, Peter J. 1980. "Typologies of Public Policy: Meaning Construction of the Policy Process." *Social Science Quarterly* 61 (September): 185-97.

Sundquist, James L. 1981. *Decline and Resurgence of Congress.* Washington, D.C.: Brookings Institution.

_____. 1968. *Politics and Policy: The Eisenhower, Kennedy, and Johnson Years.* Washington, D.C.: Brookings Institution.

Thomas, Norman C. (ed.). 1975. *Presidency in Contemporary Context.* New York: Dodd, Mead and Co.

Truman, David B. 1969. "Presidential Executives or Congressional Executives." In Aaron Wildavsky, ed., *The Presidency*, 486-91. Boston: Little, Brown.

_____. 1959. *The Congressional Party: A Case Study.* New York: John Wiley and Sons.

Uslaner, Eric, and Ronald E. Weber. 1975. "The 'Politics' of Redistribution: Toward a Model of the Policy-Making Process in the American States." *American Politics Quarterly* 3 (April): 131-69.

Vogler, David. 1977. *The Politics of Congress.* 2d ed. Boston: Allyn and Bacon.

Wayne, Stephen J. 1978. *The Legislative Presidency.* New York: Harper and Row.

Wildavsky, Aaron B. 1979. *Speaking Truth to Power.* Boston: Little, Brown.

_____. 1966. "The Two Presidencies." *Transaction* 4 (December): 7-14.

Wilson, James Q. 1973. *Political Organizations.* New York: Basic Books.

Zeidenstein, Harvey G. 1981. "The Two Presidencies Thesis Is Alive and Well and Has Been Living in the U.S. Senate Since 1973." *Presidential Studies Quarterly* 11 (Fall): 511-25.

Index

About the Author

STEVEN A SHULL is Professor of Political Science at the University of New Orleans, Louisiana. He is the author of *Interrelated Concepts in Policy Research, Presidential Policy-Making: An Analysis,* and *Presidency: Studies in Public Policy.* His articles and book chapters have appeared in *Journal of Politics, Policy-Making in the Federal Executive Branch, International Journal of Public Administration, Journal of Political Science, Western Political Quarterly, Georgia Political Science Association Journal, Policy Perspectives, National Government and Policy in the United States, Midwest* and *Southern Reviews of Public Administration, Presidential Studies Quarterly,* and *Social Science Quarterly.* Currently, he is co-editing a symposium issue on the "Presidency and Public Policy" for the *Policy Studies Journal.*